MIRACLE ON THE MAYFLOWER

John Howland's Remarkable Rescue and Lasting Impact on America

by Cynthia Howard Hogg

© Copyright 2024 by Cynthia Howard Hogg

Page Turner Press, an imprint of Exaltation Press

All rights reserved

No part of this book may be used or reproduced, distributed, or transmitted in any form or by any means, including photocopying, recording, or other electronic or mechanical methods, without the proper written permission of the publisher, except in the case of brief quotations apart, embodied in critical reviews and certain other non-commercial uses permitted by copyright law. Use of this publication is permitted solely for personal use and must include full attribution of the material's source.

Without in any way limiting the author's and publisher's exclusive rights under copyright, any use of this publication to "train" generative artificial intelligence (AI) technologies to generate text is expressly prohibited. The author reserves all rights to license uses of this work for generative AI training and development of machine learning language models.

eBook ISBN: 978-1-950067-89-3

Paperback ISBN: 978-1-950067-88-6

Hardcover ISBN: 978-1-950067-87-9

Dedicated to my family genealogists: my father, John Carson Howard, and my son, John Carson Howard Hogg; and to my husband, Robb, with gratitude for his unfailing support.

The creation of a thousand forests is in one acorn.

~ Ralph Waldo Emerson

Preface

"God created man because he likes stories."

~ Elie Wiesel, *The Gates of the Forest*

(1964 novel)

Perhaps God also plucked John Howland from a brutal Atlantic storm – and from obscurity – because he likes stories. Certainly the number of fascinating stories flowing from this one improbable rescue is enough to keep God and man entertained for a long time to come.

Table of Contents

PART ONE: THE MAN — 9
- CHAPTER 1 *Man Overboard!* — 11
- CHAPTER 2 *Before the Voyage* — 15
- CHAPTER 3 *Waiting* — 20
- CHAPTER 4 *The Rescue* — 23
- CHAPTER 5 *Providence* — 26
- CHAPTER 6 *The Separatists* — 29
- CHAPTER 7 *Enter the Grim Reaper* — 31
- CHAPTER 8 *The Teflon Saint* — 36
- CHAPTER 9 *John Howland Takes a Wife* — 40

PART TWO – THE MANY — 45
- CHAPTER 1 *Humphrey Bogart (1899 – 1957)* — 47
- CHAPTER 2 *Ralph Waldo Emerson (1803 – 1882)* — 50
- CHAPTER 3 *Henry Wadsworth Longfellow (1807 – 1882)* — 54
- CHAPTER 4 *Joseph Smith (1805 – 1844)* — 65
- CHAPTER 5 *Esther Allen Howland (1828 – 1904)* — 69
- CHAPTER 6 *Jane Austin (1831 – 1894)* — 73
- CHAPTER 7 *Phillips Brooks (1835 – 1893)* — 78
- CHAPTER 8 *Florence Earle Nicholson Coates (1850 – 1927) Alice Nicholson Coates Trask (1873 – 1955)* — 83
- CHAPTER 9 *Maude Adams (1880 – 1953)* — 86
- CHAPTER 10 *Edith Carow Roosevelt (1861 – 1948) and Her Children* — 89
- CHAPTER 11 *Franklin Delano Roosevelt (1882 – 1945)* — 99
- CHAPTER 12 *Ruth Wales du Pont (1889 – 1967)* — 116
- CHAPTER 13 *Dr. Benjamin Spock (1903 – 1998)* — 121
- CHAPTER 14 *Eville Gorham (1925 – 2020)* — 126
- CHAPTER 15 *George H. W. Bush (1924 – 2018)* — 129
- CHAPTER 16 *George W. Bush (1946 – present)* — 133

EPILOGUE — 136

A COMPENDIUM OF QUOTES — 141

PART ONE: THE MAN

Say his last name quickly three times –

Howland, Howland, Howland –

and you get a sense of the wind on that fateful day.

Chapter 1
Man Overboard!

The high-pitched wailing of the wind cloaked the whimpering of frightened children and muffled the *shushing*, the consoling words, the whispered prayers of their mothers.

It nearly, but not quite, drowned out the sound of intermittent retching.

Over and over, as walls of water slammed the ship, bits of old caulking rained down from between the planks. Icy seawater seeped in through the cracks, making the wood floor slick and treacherous.

Women and girls hiked up and knotted their damp skirts below their knees, for it was not just seawater that slickened the oak plank floor. Wooden buckets full of human waste and vomit sloshed their contents across the floor with every violent pitch of the boat.

In fair weather, the passengers were allowed up on the top deck. They took the not infrequent tauntings and insults from the crew members in stride, just for the opportunity for some fresh air and exercise. These opportunities were all too rare and now, during a violent storm, all 102 of them had been ordered to remain in the gun or "'tween deck" – the dark, dank area between the top deck and the cargo hold – until further notice.

Only 58 feet by 24 feet, with a ceiling less than 5-1/2 feet tall, this was no place for the claustrophobic. As the storm wore on, a number of adults had not stood fully upright in more than a week. The berths, cobbled together and stacked on each other, were cramped, shadowy, and damp. A thirty-foot shallop, a small single-sail boat used for landings, cramped the space even further. Some of the men wrapped themselves in blankets and made their beds there.

When they boarded the ship a month earlier, three women had not only been "with child," but well advanced in their third trimesters. One had now given birth. Three days later, the smell of blood still filled the air, along with the newborn's weak cries.

There were no portholes. Rarely did fresh air make its way down below. And that thing that nuzzled you in the dark may not be a loved one…but a rat.

There were three levels to this ship and they were the human meat in a sandwich fast turning rancid, for this was a cargo ship, never designed to carry humans other than its crew. They had been warned of the conditions before they boarded the boat, but believed they could put up with anything for the two months it would take to reach their goal. After all, "desperate times require desperate measures" and they had all experienced desperate times. They were now ready for desperate measures. They believed God would protect and sustain them as they sought to follow His will.

But now an intense desperation gripped them as a raging storm pummeled their small wooden ship, the *Mayflower*.

Gripped them until, with a shudder and a thump, a gentle rocking suddenly replaced the violent tossing. A tentative hope crept in, along with questions.

Had the storm let up? They could still hear rain beating against the wooden frame. *Why, then, this new calm? And what had caused that thump, followed by a shudder?*

A young John Howland was one of the passengers hunkered down below. He had embarked on this trip as an indentured servant to John Carver, one of the more prominent members of the Pilgrim group, and the new colony's first governor.

We have no record of John Howland's birth but historical clues place him somewhere between the ages of 18 and 28. As he was one of the signers of the Mayflower Compact at the end of the voyage in December, 1620, we know he was at least 18-21 years of age. He was literate and capable and because his duties extended well beyond those of a young servant – he also served as Carver's executive assistant and personal secretary – he may well have been closer to his mid to late 20s.

Regardless, Howland would never have ventured up to the top deck on his own, not when under the authority of two masters—his own and the ship's captain. Howland was likely sent up top by Carver to inquire about the status of the storm.

What none of the passengers below could know was that this new calm was due to the crew's decision to lower all sails and turn the boat into the wind, a "heave to," to quiet the violent tossing.

It created a deceptive lull in a still raging storm.

As a result, when John Howland pushed open the hatch and emerged on the top deck, he was bewildered by the dark sky and pouring rain, surprised by the force of the gales that pummeled him—and terrified when, with a lurch of the ship, a loose sail knocked him overboard and into the roiling waves.

Chapter 2
Before the Voyage

Just a few short weeks earlier, it had all looked so promising. William Bradford, the group's historian, recorded that they had set sail from Plymouth, England, under "a prosperous wind." Expectations of a fresh start and a better life filled their hearts as full as "the prosperous wind" filled the Mayflower's sails.

To be sure, they had weathered many a challenge to get to this point. They were Separatists, the most conservative yet non-conforming branch of the Puritans. Unwilling to reform their religious institutions from within, they separated themselves from the Church of England for matters of conscience. They found this also required them to separate themselves physically from England for the church-state connection there meant they were not just guilty of religious dissent, but treason. In the early 1600s, they emigrated to Holland, eventually settling in Leiden.

It turned out that life in Holland didn't solve their problems. It created new ones: difficult work situations, different political worries, and concerns that their children were losing their English heritage and becoming Dutch. They longed for a place where they could remain English, yet build a new society according to the dictates of their consciences.

Might this place lie across the Atlantic in the "New World," as it was being called? They would not be the first Europeans to attempt a settlement there, and previous attempts had proved disastrous in some cases. Was it worth the risk? Could they bring women and children? Should they split up families for a time? For many in their little community, the answer was *yes*.

As one of the few English Separatists who fared well in Holland, John Carver emerged as a leader. Plans for the journey began to come together, so he traveled between Holland and England to make arrangements. In England he found and purchased the twelve-year-old ship, Mayflower, a 180-tun (a tun being a large barrel) merchant ship. He left it moored in Southampton, England. Back in Holland, the group purchased a smaller sister ship, the Speedwell. That summer of 1620, the Separatists in Holland planned to travel aboard the Speedwell to England, join the group waiting there, then sail both boats across the Atlantic to start their new lives.

Their careful plans began to go awry almost immediately.

The most significant problem involved the *Speedwell* which did not, well, speed well. Twice the *Mayflower* and the *Speedwell* set out on their journey together, those onboard waving hankies to their friends and loved ones waiting on shore to see them off. Twice they returned to English ports when the *Speedwell* began leaking.

Why was the *Speedwell* leaking? Apparently something nefarious was going on.

The Pilgrims had raised money to buy the Speedwell, not just for the trip across the Atlantic, but to keep in the New World for transportation and trading purposes. They had hired the crew to stay with them throughout the first year. The *Mayflower*, on the other hand, had been hired just for the initial trip and ship and crew were supposed to return to England soon after depositing the Pilgrims in the New World.

As delays pushed the departure for both ships to a later date, the crew of the *Speedwell* began to grow nervous. They had legitimate concerns about the depletion of necessary provisions during the delays (some sold off to pay debts and some used by the Pilgrims waiting on board) and the prospect of now traveling during rougher weather. These fears were compounded by tales they had heard about the "Starving Times" in the New World, the high rates of illness and death – and even stories of settlers resorting to cannibalism and eating their own shoes to survive. They didn't have the same motivation as the Pilgrims to start a "brave new world." Suddenly the prospect of spending a year with these "religious fanatics" in a forbidding wilderness no longer seemed that attractive.

And so they set about to scuttle the voyage of the *Speedwell* by purposefully sabotaging the ship. Some historians think they did it through "overmasting" (using a bigger mast than necessary), which put strain on the hull. Others think they directly damaged some of the planks so that the ship began leaking, without actually sinking. Either way, the Pilgrims were forced to sell the *Speedwell* at an auction at great financial loss. Interestingly, the new owners used the ship for many successful voyages, without incident.

The crew of the *Speedwell* happily moved on to a new project, but what of its passengers? Some decided they had just had too much and elected to stay behind. Still others were "encouraged" to do so because the space was now so limited.

The remainder crammed onto the *Mayflower*.

A further difficulty of note had greeted the Leiden group when they first arrived in England. The company financially underwriting much of the journey, referred to as "The Merchant Adventurers," had added a rather large group of passengers who had very little in common with the religious or political views of the Separatists. The Pilgrims had not counted on this. A tight-knit group bound together by their faith who, above all else, strove to live up to the name they called each other – "Saints" – they were aghast at sharing such close quarters with these "Strangers," as they called them, especially since many of the Separatists were traveling with their young children.

Well, they would draw close together, and protect and support each other. They had done it before.

Frictions began well before they set sail. With nowhere else to go, many of the Pilgrims moved onto the *Mayflower* and lived there for a month while the *Speedwell* was being prepared for the journey. They staked out claims to the best places, erecting partitions and hanging up curtains. They also lived off of some of the rations meant for the trip. None of this went over well when the "Strangers," who boarded the boat a month later.

When they finally set off together, they were 102 passengers, plus a crew of about thirty. On the surface, everything looked like smooth sailing: bright sunshine and calm seas. Below the surface, it was a different story. The cramped quarters, tensions among the passengers, and reduced rations did not bode well for long-term success. Although the crew surely was aware, the passengers likely did not fully realize how the many delays would impact them, especially in terms of the weather. Instead of sailing as originally planned during July, August, and September, their departure in September would place the bulk of their journey during the unpredictable months of October and November.

Chapter 3
Waiting

The churning waves hit John Howland like an icy hammer as he plummeted down, down, his woolen pants and heavy boots – once his friends against the elements but now his enemies – filled with water.

He flailed. He grasped, but came up with nothing. Which way was up? He couldn't tell as he spun underwater.

Waiting.

So much of his life thus far had consisted of waiting. Waiting for a life of adventure and purpose outside his small hometown of Fenstanton, north of London. Waiting in Leiden, Holland, while the Separatist leaders made their plans for a journey to the New World. Waiting onboard the ship for a month while repairs were completed. After two aborted attempts to set sail, waiting in the hold of a stinking, rat-infested ship. Looking down the road—waiting for the completion of his term as an indentured servant so he could be a free man, his own man. *Finally.*

Now, instead, in the frigid waters of the Atlantic, he waited to die.

Like a soldier dying on a battlefield, did his final thoughts turn to his mother back in England? She would be waiting too; waiting for word from him that he had arrived safely in the New World. It would be months. Christmas would come and go. Long after his bones lay on the ocean floor, swaddled in unfulfilled dreams, she would still be thinking of him, praying for him – not knowing.

He continued to flail. His lungs burned as he held his breath against the salty brine swirling around him.

Then, in the surging, stormy sea, something hard and rough whacked against his body. It stunned him, but just for a moment, before recognition and a renewed hope dawned.

Whack! There it was again. *A rope.*

His icy fingers managed to grab a hold of the rope and he held onto it with all his strength.

When the crew lowered the sails during their "heave to," it left the topsail halyard dragging in the water beside the boat. Although William Bradford recorded in his journal that John Howland remained underwater "for some fathoms" when he found the rope, somehow he was able to hang on and painfully pull himself up against the drag of the water until he broke the surface.

His pent-up breath exploded from him. He gasped, "Help!" but the wind swallowed up his plea.

The storm still beating against him, his heavy wet clothes dragging him down, his hands raw and bleeding, he lacked the superhuman strength needed to pull himself up the remaining thirty feet of rope and over the railing.

"Help me!" he cried and once again, the wind flung his words back at him.

No faces appeared at the railing to assist him.

Waiting, once again.

Chapter 4
The Rescue

Several of the crew saw him swept overboard—saw him and had a decision to make. A rescue would not be easy. The deck was slippery. Hanging over the railing, pulling on a rope, the boat rocking and pitching, storm-surged waves could just as easily sweep them overboard also. Besides, he was one of *them*, and only an indentured servant, nobody important enough to risk their lives for.

And yet, they acted.

We can only speculate about what motivated them. As an indentured servant, John Howland was under authority, just as they were, a working-class kindred spirit. Just days earlier, a savage wave had proved too much for one of the main structural timbers of the ship. The damage was so severe it caused even the ship's master to consider turning back. It was the Saints who urged them to push on. They dug out a screw jack they'd brought to help assemble houses in the new land. Working together, they repaired the timber and the journey continued. Young and strong, unencumbered by a wife and children, John Howland might well have helped with the repair.

Had he earned the grudging respect of the crew by so doing?

Did he instantly become "one of them" the minute he was swept overboard, where in any battle between man and the bully sea, sailors unite to prevail against the latter?

Or might it have had something to do with the death of one of their own just a few days earlier? William Bradford gives us the account of this sailor's death:

And I may mention here a special work of God's providence. There was a proud and very profane young man; one of the seamen, of a lusty, able body, which made him the more haughty; he would always be condemning the poor people in their sickness, and cursing them daily with grievous execrations, and told them, that he hoped to help to cast half of them overboard before they came to their journey's end, and to make merry with what they had; and if he were by any gently reproved, he would curse and swear most bitterly. But it pleased God before they came half seas over, to smite this young man with a grievous disease, of which he died in a desperate manner, and so was himself the first that was thrown overboard. Thus, his curses fell on his own head; and it was an astonishment to all his fellows, for they noted it to be the just hand of God upon him.

Sailors tend to be a superstitious lot. Perhaps their comrade's death stirred up a dormant fear of God among them.

Whatever their reasons, they swung into action. John Howland held fast to the rope and hand over hand, a small group of sailors pulled him halfway up the rough side of the ship. Then, when they had him close enough, several others snagged him with a large boat hook and yanked him up and over the railing to safety, beyond the clutches of the grasping sea.

    At least for the moment.

CHAPTER 5
Providence

Quickly bundled back down the hatch and stripped of his clothes, Howland found himself in the awkward position of having nothing to wear. With no space onboard to wash clothes, and no real means to do so, the passengers had been told they were to wear the same set of clothes the entire journey.

Now his single set of clothes lay in a sodden heap. How long would it take them to dry in this dark, damp place? Dripping wet, shivering, trying to shake off despair, Howland waited while his friends scrambled to find something dry to wrap him in.

As he waited, details of his rescue rippled through the crowded quarters, the incredible story whispered from person to person. Almost imperceptibly at first, the dark mood of the last week or two began to give way to something different, for Howland was viewed as dripping not just with seawater but with something far more important: the favor of Almighty God.

For the Pilgrims, there was no luck, good or bad—only Providence. The question hung in the air: Would God provide such a miraculous rescue, only to have this young man perish later in the voyage? What would be the sense in that? No, this rescue must be a favorable sign. God was with this young indentured servant and by extension, with them all.

Just as Howland had clung to the topsail halyard for hope of survival, his fellow passengers must now have clung to his rescue as a sign of their ultimate survival. Since God plucked John Howland from the roiling, stormy seas, there must be a Reason. If there was a Reason, then they were not going to perish.

And with this rescue so closely juxtaposed to the death on board just a few days earlier? Haughty and profane, the sailor had been struck with a dread disease and quickly died, his body cast overboard into the sea. Now, one of their own – pious, hard-working and humble – had been pulled from that same sea in a rescue nothing short of miraculous. Had God not just clearly demonstrated for them both his justice and his mercy?

Heaving, creaking, leaking, damp and cramped, this cargo-vessel-turned-passenger-ship no longer seemed like a death trap to the Saints and Strangers onboard. Instead, like Noah's Ark of ancient times, it rocked secure in the palm of God's hand, anointed with Purpose.

John Howland must have felt it too as he lay shivering in his bunk, borrowed blankets and the belongings of friends banked around him for extra warmth. It must have seeped into his heart, his bones, and warmed him more than the blankets, buoying him and giving him strength – this knowledge that, against great odds, the hand of God had protected and restored him to his friends.

It only remained for him to discover the reason why.

Chapter 6
The Separatists

They were the original Hippies—long-haired, non-conformists, anti-establishment. They gave their children names like Love (a boy), and Desire (a girl), and Wrestling (another boy).

Wrestling?

Presumably wrestling with doubts or the devil, and hoping to prevail.

We know how they landed at Plymouth Rock in December of 1620, but whatever else we *think* we know, is likely nothing more than myths and misconceptions.

For one thing, they were not Puritans, as they are sometimes incorrectly called. The Puritans were the ones who stayed in England and remained within the Church. Because they wanted to purify the Church from within – hence the name *Puritans* – they were extremely strict and severe.

In a sense, no "Pilgrims" left England in 1620 for they weren't called Pilgrims at the time, nor did they think of themselves as such. The name "Pilgrims" was not applied to them until two hundred years later when others considered they had embarked on a "pilgrimage" to find a new home. They thought of themselves as Separatists, separating themselves from the Church they knew, and determined to create something better.

Subtract the idea of "free love" and you might have found this idealistic, yet slightly naïve, bunch at home in a commune in the 1960s.

They had a good sense of humor. They liked their beer.

They did not dress in black and white, with large buckles on their shoes and hats, despite the countless elementary school age children so decked out in annual Thanksgiving programs. Many in this group dressed in greens, and bright blues and purples, even velvets and silks.

And finally, they did not land at Plymouth Rock, all disembark, and get to work building a new colony. Many of them, especially the women and children, continued to live on the Mayflower for several more months, rocking in the harbor, buffeted by winter winds, waiting and praying.

Chapter 7
Enter the Grim Reaper

The first land spotted from the Mayflower was the narrow, curved arm of Cape Cod. This was not where they hoped to be. The crew tried to head south to their original destination of Virginia, but were forced to turn back. It was just too late in the season, so they resigned themselves to starting a new life where God had brought them. Cold weather had set in, and was only going to get colder. They needed to quickly begin building shelters and they desperately needed food.

They also needed to get off the cramped and disease-ridden Mayflower.

The Mayflower had started off the journey to the New World as a "sweet ship," so called because for years it had transported wine between France and England. The inevitable spillage soaked into the wooden floorboards to create a lingering pleasant odor. But on this voyage, with its first animal and human cargo and their attendant waste, it didn't remain a sweet ship for long.

The men onboard, passengers and crew members, hauled the shallop up from the middle deck, quickly worked to reassemble and repair it after it had been used as a bed, and lowered it over the side of the Mayflower. They assembled a small scouting party of ten passengers and eight crew to explore this exciting but strange new land. They returned with some very welcome berries and small game, but with no news of a place to build. They set out again, and again, a total of three times.

Danger stalked them at every turn.

Snap! A startled William Bradford, snatched in mid-step, dangled nearly upside down when caught in a deer trap laid by the local Native people. The other men in the scouting party cut him down and they continued on their way.

Swoosh! An arrow flew past their heads, sending the men scrambling for the shallop. Who could blame the Native people? Several previous encounters with Europeans had not ended well.

Splash! A sudden winter squall swamped their small boat. The men were able to save it and reach safety on a nearby island, but now their sodden clothes were frozen to their shivering bodies.

At last, on the mainland high above Plymouth Harbor, they found the spot they had been looking for. They were not the first humans to desire this spot, nor did they have to clear it first to make it habitable. In an ironic twist, they began building on a spot prepared by earlier Europeans who had cleared the land not with axes, but by accidentally introducing smallpox to the Patuxet Indians who lived there. If they had known this spot had been cleared for them by Death, might they have kept looking for a different spot? But they didn't know, so they happily embraced it.

The men returned to the ship to share their good news.

The Pilgrims aboard the ship had news too.

Who would have guessed that staying on the ship – anchored safely in the harbor, sheltered from winter storms, dwindling food rations nevertheless close at hand – would prove deadlier than the men's rowing through ice-clogged waters, slogging through snow and sleet, and encountering Indians?

Through all these dangers, the scouting parties had lost not one man, nor suffered a single serious injury. Although often cold, hungry, and exhausted, they had the advantage of sunshine, fresh air, fresh water to drink, exercise – and distance from the spreading illnesses onboard.

Perhaps these mundane advantages kept the Grim Reaper from joining their scouting expeditions. Perhaps it was the presence of the God-anointed John Howland among their number that kept him at bay.

Or perhaps the Grim Reaper was so busy onboard he hadn't time to bother with the men on shore.

Unseen, he had slipped aboard the boat, hiding behind the shallop at first, then behind the barrels of English water, now grown slimy. He played in the shadows with the rats.

As the weeks dragged on, he grew bolder, stepped out of the shadows, and leered at them.

During the voyage, William Butten, a young servant boy of about 14, had been the first to die.

Poor little lad. No real family to mourn him. No real place to bury him, so they lowered his cold body into the icy waters of the Atlantic.

His death was sad, but not tragic. Though mourned, he was not a key member of the group.

But when the scouting party returned from their third and most successful scouting expedition, news of a different kind of death awaited them. Just days before, a key woman had joined the young servant boy in his watery grave: 23-year-old Dorothy Bradford, wife of William Bradford, the colony's historian and later, their longest-serving governor. Dorothy had slipped on the icy deck, fallen overboard, and drowned in the frigid waters of Provincetown Harbor.

Did any of the others see her fall overboard and despair when they were unable to rescue her? Or did it happen while she was alone? Was the weather calm, or did she lose her footing during a winter storm? We don't know. William Bradford kept good records of the journey and the founding of "Plimouth Plantation," but he recorded nothing about his wife's death.

Her death must have sent a chill through the group far more gripping than any winter storm.

She was one of them, a God-fearing woman. A young mother, whose three-year-old son waited back in Holland for her to send for him. He would never see her again. She had prayed with them, encouraged them, helped care for the other small children on board. Now she was gone, claimed by the dark and forbidding waters that still surrounded their ship. Hoping to mitigate the grief of her death somewhat with the good news of finding a spot for their permanent settlement, they pulled up anchor and moved the ship from Provincetown Harbor to their new location of Plymouth Harbor.

If Dorothy's death seemed like a bad omen to some in the group, they did not lose it by changing locations. Almost immediately, a "great sickness" took hold.

The exact nature of the sickness is unknown. Some historians suspect it was pneumonia. Certainly, malnutrition and scurvy contributed to the mortality rates. In his records, Bradford referred to the next few months as "The Starving Time." The women exhausted themselves cooking and caring for the sick and, one by one, they also began to die.

Bradford did not record all the deaths. He may not have had the strength or time but we know that between January and March, they lost Rose Standish, Mary Allerton, (who had given birth to a stillborn son just ten weeks earlier), and Elizabeth Winslow.

Men and children were dying too.

The healthy men struggled to first build a "common house" so they could clear out the boat and store some of their supplies. But in early January, the common house caught fire. They were able to contain the fire but not put it out before the entire structure burned to the ground.

The flames were visible from the ship. As those on board huddled on deck and watched yet another dream turn to literal ashes, it must have been impossible to quench this burning question: *had God abandoned them*?

Chapter 8
The Teflon Saint

It has been observed, "Adversity introduces a man to himself." It's also true that adversity introduces one to the character of others. At first, the ship's master ordered all the sick off his ship – an inhumane and ultimately impossible request when people were gravely ill and the conditions outside the ship were so harsh. And transport them to where? The common house had burned down in mid-January, and sometimes, only three or four adult men were healthy enough at any one time to continue building anything. The ship's master, Christopher Jones, also refused to give the passengers any of the food onboard, stating it was needed for the return voyage. There was no way that the passengers, even if healthy, could have foraged enough food to feed a hundred people.

At one point, only seven adults and a few children were healthy enough to care for nearly a hundred others. (Bradford recorded that there were a few others healthy enough to help but who initially refused, afraid to get sick themselves.) The amount of work was unimaginable, even if the weather had been more favorable. The constant scourging for enough food and for firewood to keep the fires going; the cooking, serving and washing up; the tending to the sick and trying to bury the dead; it was endless and back breaking. "The Great Sickness" and "The Starving Time" were decimating their numbers.

The ship's master eventually relented when his own crew began to fall sick, and the whole group pulled together more. William Bradford did not record his young wife's death but he must have felt her loss deeply for he fell deathly ill soon after and was not expected to live. It was Myles Standish, a gruff soldier and "Stranger," who nursed him back to health. They became lifelong friends, despite their very different backgrounds. One of the ship's crew, who had been cruel and insulting to the Saints, became devoted to them after they nursed him back to health. If at the beginning of the voyage there were Saints and Strangers and crew members, three distinct groups, by the end of the first winter there existed just one frail group, bound together by a need to survive.

By March, the worst of it was over but only half of the original passengers and crew had survived.

In April, the sun came out, warming the land and warming their hearts. The *Mayflower* returned to England, its crew skeletal in more ways than one. The ship's master offered free passage to any Saint or Stranger who wanted to return with him. Not one surviving passenger accepted his offer.

Hope had returned, its tiny, tender roots taking hold in this foreign soil. How could they now abandon it?

Then a dark cloud appeared that April. Whereas they had experienced between sixty and seventy deaths during the winter, only four more occurred throughout the remainder of the year.

But two of those were significant.

John Carver, the Governor of the new colony of Plymouth, and his wife, Katherine, had both survived the winter, no small feat when so many others had succumbed. But after that unusually cold winter, in an ironic twist of fate, Governor John Carver died of apparent sunstroke.

In April. Barely into spring.

William Bradford recorded that after laboring all day to prepare his fields in the long-awaited warmth, Carver staggered toward his home, collapsed, and died later that same day. His death sent shock waves through the shock-weary colony.

Katherine followed her husband in death a few short weeks later. Bradford recorded that she died of a "broken heart."

Although she no doubt remained weak from lack of food throughout the winter, who can doubt she died of a broken heart? For months, she had endured some of the most challenging conditions imaginable. After burying two children in Holland, she boarded the Mayflower deeply mired in grief, but still clinging to hopes of a better life. She survived the perilous voyage, lived hand-to-mouth for months, never enough to eat, a constant struggle to keep from freezing. She watched her intimate friends die around her, one by one. *Each death like a hammer blow.* Still, she persevered. She had her husband. He was strong, important, the governor of this fledgling colony that had sacrificed so much. She believed in him. Believed in what they were doing. Believed they had a future.

Now it was all gone. No husband. No children. Most of her close friends dead. What did she have to live for? Suddenly it must have all seemed pointless, hopeless. When she buried her husband, she must have felt she had buried any dream of future happiness. No wonder her soul and body gave out.

In the midst of all this stood their indentured servant: the Teflon Pilgrim, John Howland, to whom nothing tragic seemed to stick.

The Grim Reaper dogged him at every turn, but Howland stared him down, refusing to flinch. He survived the rough voyage and near drowning. He survived the initial landing on Cape Cod when, as a member of each scouting party, he explored the rugged, unfamiliar terrain. He survived a surprise attack by Indians. And that dark first winter, as illness and death swept through the group, John Howland again emerged unscathed.

Was anyone surprised?

Chapter 9
John Howland Takes a Wife

The problem with historical figures is just that. They often become figures, stick figures, two-dimensional with all of the life sucked out of them. They come to us through written descriptions, and sometimes pictures, also flat and two-dimensional. Of course, it has to be this way. Once a person dies or is removed from us by several generations, words and pictures are all that's left…and sometimes we're lucky to have even those.

Only in our imaginations is it possible to breathe life back into them, making them flesh and blood again, as we ponder the dynamics behind the flat, written words.

The hardships and illnesses that decimated their numbers broke down more than barriers between classes and different groups; it broke down family units. In some cases, whole families were wiped out. In others, a single member or several members survived. For purposes of safety and provision, a constant reshuffling ensued.

Young Elizabeth Tilley, 13 at the time, lost both of her parents, John and Joan Tilley, that first winter. She also lost her aunt and uncle, Edward and Ann Tilley. She found shelter in the home of John and Katherine Carver. A few months later, when Carver died of sunstroke and Katherine soon followed, Elizabeth found herself once again an orphan and on her own.

But only technically, for now John Howland, the former indentured servant, had become a free man. It is speculated (but unproven) that he also inherited some of the Carver estate, as there were no immediate heirs. He kept the small house they were living in, and took over the role of head of the household, which now contained the orphaned Elizabeth Tilley, who became his ward, a young woman named Desire Minter, and a young servant boy named William Latham. Not one of them was related to another by blood, but together they formed a kind of family unit.

How interesting the dynamics must have been. Desire was three years older than Elizabeth. She was the daughter of English Separatists in Holland, sent with the Carvers on the Mayflower when her mother remarried. What must it have been like for them, living in such close quarters? The houses were tiny, just one or two rooms. John Howland was certainly an eligible bachelor, with his new freedom and land and house. By 1623, Howland was granted an acre of land for himself and each of the other three in his home, including the servant boy. By now, Elizabeth was 16, Desire 19, both of marriageable age. How odd that the community let these girls remain, unchaperoned, in the home of an unmarried young man.

By all accounts, the girls became fast friends. In their small circle there was also Henry Sampson, 19, who had been left without a family when his aunt and uncle – also Elizabeth's aunt and uncle – died during the first winter. Elizabeth might have been expected to marry Henry, a cousin by marriage. In a time and place where courtship was driven as much by survival as romance, Desire and Henry, the same age, might also have been thought a good match.

But Elizabeth Tilley did not marry her cousin. Perhaps she had come to doubt the strength of the Tilley constitution after burying all four Tilley adults soon after their arrival in Plymouth. In close proximity to John Howland, watching how he handled things and mindful of his God-pleasing rescue, was it any wonder she wanted to cast her lot in with him instead?

Desire did not marry either of these young men, or anyone else. Instead, she eventually returned to England sometime after 1623. It likely had nothing to do with a broken heart.

There were plenty of other reasons.

At that first Thanksgiving feast in the autumn of 1621, very few women and young girls remained alive to help with the cooking and festivities. Elizabeth Tilley was listed among the helpers. Desire Minter was not, listed instead as "sickly."

What did "sickly" mean exactly? Had her health never quite recovered from the previous winter? Or was it something more? There is an emotional starvation that can eat away at a person every bit as brutally as the emptiness in a stomach. In the depth of winter, the ground grew harder, the graves shallower. Did each new *clang* of a shovel on the frozen earth jar her world? She had been a young girl when she left her mother back in Holland. How many of the women in the group had become like second mothers to her?

And how many of them had she now buried?

Her own mother, twice widowed, had remarried a third time and was more settled. Did Desire long to return to her mother now, to feel her embrace as she stroked Desire's hair and murmured, *"It's all right, dear—you're warm now and have enough to eat"*? Perhaps she also longed for marriage. There certainly existed a wider pool of eligible prospects back in England. Finding herself between a rock (Plymouth Rock) and a hard place (stepping back onboard a despised ship to recross the perilous ocean), Desire chose the latter.

Only two young female passengers on the Mayflower ever returned to England. One was Humility Cooper, also a Tilley cousin, who was just a toddler. She had no say in the matter. The other was Desire Minter. Sadly, both of these young girls died after their return to England, neither having lived long enough to marry or leave a legacy.

All of the young girls who stayed in Plymouth married, had large families, and lived to an advanced age.

Life is an interesting puzzle.

Elizabeth Tilley, bereft of all family, remained in Plymouth and married John Howland in 1623, at the tender age of sixteen. At night, they lay huddled together on a narrow bed in a narrow room. They listened to the wind whistle through the cracks in the walls and the wolves howl outside their door. They found comfort and strength in each other, and the begetting and begatting began.

Their first child was a daughter.

They named her Desire.

PART TWO – THE MANY

Here's Looking at You, Kid(s)

Chapter 1

Humphrey Bogart (1899 – 1957)

At least two million: the estimated number of U. S. citizens descended from John and Elizabeth Tilley Howland in fewer than sixteen generations. This is considered a conservative estimate. Some believe it may be upwards of ten million.

John and Elizabeth started with ten: six girls and four boys. The number is not as remarkable as the fact that, considering the times, all ten survived into adulthood, married, and had children of their own. An average of 8.8 children each. Yes, *each,* providing John and Elizabeth with eighty-eight grandchildren.

Not a bad start in the New World.

The oldest daughter, Desire, bested her parents by one by having eleven children, as did her sister Elizabeth and brother Jabez. Brother John equaled his parents with ten. Hannah and Joseph each had nine and Isaac had eight. Hope held the record with twelve children. Only Ruth, with three, and Lydia, with four, were slackers in comparison.

Although no doubt leading busy and interesting lives, the vast majority of John Howland descendants are unknown outside their own little circles. Other descendants have recognizable names, having made their marks and enjoyed various degrees of fame and influence.

Still others have changed the world.

The mix of names includes politicians like Nathaniel Gorham, president of the Continental Congress and signer of the U.S. Constitution; Governor and Vice-Presidential candidate Sarah Palin; Senator and U.S. Ambassador to the United Nations, Henry Cabot Lodge II; First Lady Edith Carow Roosevelt; and Presidents Franklin Delano Roosevelt, George Herbert Walker Bush, and George W. Bush. It also includes authors Ralph Waldo Emerson and Henry Wadsworth Longfellow; religious leaders Phillips Brooks and Joseph Smith; and actors Alec and Stephen Baldwin, Christopher Lloyd, Lillian Russell, Maude Adams, and Humphrey Bogart.

Aah, Humphrey Bogart.

Born into privilege, he dashed his parents' dreams of Yale and a distinguished career by getting kicked out of elite private schools, joining the Navy at eighteen, and forging an acting career where he rose to fame as a hard-bitten tough guy.

When he speaks in the movies, his lips barely move, but when they do, the lines are memorable. His line from *Casablanca*, "Here's looking at you, kid" is ranked fifth on the list of one hundred best cinematic quotes of all time. He has four more in the top one hundred: three from *Casablanca* and one from *The Maltese Falcon*. Over his nearly thirty-year career, he appeared in seventy-five feature films, starring in many of them.

Like his ancestor, John Howland, Bogart had a connection with the sea and longed for adventure and new horizons. He didn't see much action in the Navy during World War I, but did get to visit Paris when he wound up ferrying troops back from Europe. Unlike his ancestor, his escape from drowning proved less complete—his amidst a sea of alcohol. Overwhelmed by his many years of hard living, his body succumbed to esophageal cancer shortly after his fifty-seventh birthday.

He weighed a mere eighty pounds at the time.

Let us remember instead his soulful eyes, betraying vulnerability as well as grit; his distinctive voice; his movie lines that have become a part of our cultural fabric.

In 1991, the American Film Institute ranked Humphrey Bogart as the top male cinematic star of all time.

CHAPTER 2

Ralph Waldo Emerson (1803 – 1882)

Emerson once said, "Men are what their mothers made them." For Emerson, this is more true than he knew, in the case of his mitochondrial DNA. For those unfamiliar with the science of it, mitochondrial DNA is inherited only from one's mother, making it different from nuclear DNA, which is a mix received from mother and father. Emerson's mitochondrial DNA can be traced through an all-female line all the way back to Elizabeth Tilley of the Mayflower.

For the millions of descendants of Elizabeth Tilley Howland, there are not many who can make that claim.

Emerson said many more things, for he is the most widely quoted American of all time, more so than John F. Kennedy, Martin Luther King Jr., FDR, Maya Angelou and George Washington, combined. Most Americans have no doubt quoted him, without even knowing it:

Hitch your wagon to a star.

The only way to have a friend is to be one.

You cannot do a kindness too soon, for you never know how soon it will be too late.

Who you are speaks so loudly I can't hear what you're saying.

What lies behind us and what lies before us are tiny matters… compared to what lies within us.

But Emerson's impact on American thought and culture foes far deeper than his Hallmark-esque quotes.

Born in 1803, Emerson was a philosopher, essayist, and lecturer. He lived and died within the confines of the nineteenth century, but his influence never remained there. Well-known and well-regarded literary critic Harold Bloom (1930-2019) was a devout Emerson fan who has written extensively about Emerson's ongoing impact on American culture.

In Emerson's early position as a Unitarian minister, he trod along the outskirts of traditional Christianity before, following his own advice of *"Do not go where the path may lead, go instead where there is no path and leave a trail,"* he veered off in a direction that left orthodox Christianity behind entirely. God with a capital "G" became lowercase god and resided a little lower than the heavens – primarily in and through nature, with the altar of worship contained within oneself.

Emerson did not write in a linear way, but as one wandering through nature, observing, speaking out loud, maybe to no one in particular, a stream of consciousness recorded for others. Part of his genius was the ability to take deep, pithy ideas and sum them up in a memorable line or two.

Money often costs too much.

People wish to be settled; only as far as they are unsettled is there any hope for them.

A whole book could be written on the wisdom summed up in just those two.

He once said of his friend Margaret Fuller, *"She wore this circle of friends, when I first knew her, as a necklace of diamonds about her neck."*

A beautiful image: pure poetry.

The friends were their mutual ones in an informally organized group known today as 'The Transcendental Club,' although they never called themselves that. Emerson was considered the unofficial leader of the group. A central tenet of Transcendentalism is the belief that each person is inherently good and uniquely gifted with unlimited potential. What each individual knows "transcends" what they learn from the world through their senses; therefore, intuition and imagination, not reason, lead to truth.

In addition to working with Margaret on their Transcendentalist publication, *The Dial*, Emerson rubbed shoulders with many of the important authors of the day, including Henry Wadsworth Longfellow, Bronson Alcott, Nathaniel Hawthorne, and Henry David Thoreau. Historian Van Wyck Brooks refers to this time, roughly between 1815-1865, as "The Flowering of New England." It was the beginning of America moving away from the influence of European culture, and developing more of its own unique culture in terms of music, art, and literature. Emerson was a huge champion of this movement, once writing, *"We have listened too long to the courtly Muses of Europe."*

Their movement stressed the importance of art, literature, music and nature, but in a uniquely American form.

It stressed the individual, over against government, traditional social institutions, and organized religion.

It stressed the importance of self-reliance.

Their beliefs also formed a basis for pushing forward civil rights, including the end of slavery.

Henry David Thoreau was greatly influenced by Emerson's writings, and tried to live them out in various social experiments like the one at Walden Pond (built on Emerson's property). Together, they wrote against materialism and excess, which they saw all around them. Emerson's line, *"Can anything be so elegant as to have few wants, and to serve them one's self?"* is the perfect summary of the minimalist lifestyle so many are trying to return to today. Although it wasn't enough to entirely forestall the coming tide of robber barons and greedy industrialists, it may have tempered it somewhat, a necessary balance for their times – and our own.

While his writings contributed to an American spirit of optimism, as expressed in the following lines, *"No great man ever complains of want of opportunity"* and *"America is another name for opportunity,"* his ideas, even within his own lifetime, spread well beyond American borders.

It is reported that a 17-year-old Friedrich Nietzche devoured Emerson's writings.

Chapter 3

Henry Wadsworth Longfellow (1807 – 1882)

Henry Wadsworth Longfellow, a contemporary and fellow associate in the Transcendental Club, rose to Emerson's call to write works with uniquely American themes. In *Evangeline, Song of Hiawatha, The Courtship of Miles Standish,* and *The Midnight Ride of Paul Revere*, he presented these themes in a thrilling and romantic way that appealed to the masses.

Our image of Longfellow today is of a grandfatherly man with long, flowing white hair and beard. This image appeared on postage stamps in both 1940 and 2007. At his funeral, Emerson described him as a "sweet and beautiful soul." Throughout his life, he was described in the same way: gentle, sweet-natured, disciplined. For his life motto he adopted the Latin phrase *non clamor sed amor,* which translates to "not loudness but love."

Few realize, however, that beneath the flowing white beard,

Longfellow bore actual physical scars of a personal tragedy so deep that it almost killed him, and that his gentle heart had been pierced not once, but twice, by the most intimate kind of loss.

From the time he was a young boy, Longfellow knew he wanted to be a poet. He showed great promise while still in his teens, entering Bowdoin College at fourteen. After graduation, he traveled throughout Europe, attending lectures, taking courses, reading, writing, and teaching himself languages. He would eventually master a dozen.

As a musician, as well as a poet and linguist, he recognized his need of connecting with real people outside of his book learning. In between lectures and classes, he sought out interactions with "the common man." Basically an introvert in many ways, he used his love of music to connect with others, often striking up interactions by playing his silver flute.

Three thoughts penned by him best sum up this time in his life:

Music is the universal language of mankind.

The love of learning, the sequestered nooks, and all the sweet serenity of books.

A single conversation across the table with a wise man is better than ten years mere study of books.

When he returned to America, he became a professor of modern languages at his alma mater, writing his own textbooks based on his travels and studies. When he was offered a similar position at Harvard, it came with the stipulation that he first return to Europe for a year of further study. *What bliss!*

More bliss! He had married in the meantime, and he and his young wife, Mary, set sail together. Soon she was expecting their first child.

After their travels, he looked forward to returning to Boston with his new little family, and taking up his position at Harvard.

He and Mary did return to Boston, but not together. Mary preceded him by several months, embalmed in a lead-lined oak coffin. She had suffered a miscarriage in her sixth month of pregnancy, lingered a few weeks, then died of complications. Longfellow fell into a deep depression, writing, *"One thought occupies me night and day... She is dead – She is dead! All day I am weary and sad."*

At the conclusion of his travels, he returned to Cambridge alone, rented rooms close to Harvard in a house once used as a headquarters for George Washington, and threw himself into writing and teaching.

In 1843, he married Fanny Appleton and his long-desired "happy hearth and home" at last blossomed around him. Although they lost one daughter, he and Fanny went on to have two sons and three other daughters. A popular professor, the Longfellows' home became a lively social center for students and prominent literary figures of the day.

In 1854, Longfellow stepped down from his teaching at Harvard to devote himself to writing full time. Over the next seven years, Longfellow watched his children, his literary career, and his reputation all grow by leaps and bounds. By 1860, he had published *Hyperion*, *Evangeline*, and *The Song of Hiawatha*, along with other well-received poetry collections and translations.

Longfellow did not often bring his personal life into his writing but in 1860, he let the public have a little peek at the domestic scene which brought him so much pleasure when he published the following touching poem, "The Children's Hour."

Between the dark and the daylight,
When the night is beginning to lower,
Comes a pause in the day's occupations,
That is known as the Children's Hour.

I hear in the chamber above me
The patter of little feet,
The sound of a door that is opened,
And voices soft and sweet.

From my study I see in the lamplight,
Descending the broad hall stair,
Grave Alice, and laughing Allegra,
And Edith with golden hair.

A whisper, and then a silence:
Yet I know by their merry eyes
They are plotting and planning together
To take me by surprise.

A sudden rush from the stairway,
A sudden raid from the hall!
By three doors left unguarded
They enter my castle wall!

They climb up into my turret

O'er the arms and back of my chair;
If I try to escape, they surround me;
They seem to be everywhere.

They almost devour me with kisses,
Their arms about me entwine,
Till I think of the Bishop of Bingen
In his Mouse-Tower on the Rhine!

Do you think, o blue-eyed banditi,
Because you have scaled the wall,
Such an old mustache as I am
Is not a match for you all!

I have you fast in my fortress,
And will not let you depart,
But put you down into the dungeon
In the round-tower of my heart.

And there will I keep you forever,
Yes, forever and a day,
Till the walls shall crumble to ruin,
And moulder in dust away!

The poem contained the real names and descriptions of his three adored young daughters. Little did he realize as he penned these lines that tragedy would soon smash the idyllic family life reflected in his poetry like a hammer taken to a large mirror.

Longfellow loved children, and had a special kinship with them. In the opening line of his poem "The Village Blacksmith," a reference is made to "a spreading chestnut-tree." Everyone knew this line was inspired by a favorite tree not far from Longfellow's home. When the tree had to be cut down, children in Cambridge gathered pennies to pay for a chair fashioned out of the wood. They presented the chair to him on his 72nd birthday. According to a newspaper clipping at the time, it was quite an ornate chair, with glass ball casters, green leather seat and armrests, and much carving of the wood. Afterward, he wrote a poem called *From My Arm-Chair*, which he published "for the children of Cambridge," to show his great thanks.

How ironic, how tragic then, that Longfellow lost both of his wives through misfortunes connected to children.

His first wife, Mary, died in childbirth.

Then Fanny died in a second tragedy.

On July 9, 1861, Fanny Longfellow was in the library with her two youngest daughters. She was attempting to seal envelopes containing clippings of her children's hair. No doubt the clippings included some from "Edith with the golden hair," immortalized in the poem published the year before. A simple task, one any mother can relate to, but somehow the hot wax dripped onto Fanny's dress and ignited it and she was quickly engulfed in flames. In agony from her burns, she suffered through the night before dying the next morning. Longfellow, who tried to smother the flames with a rug, suffered serious burns to his face and hands. Unable to shave because of the scars, he grew out his long white beard, so much a part of his image ever since.

A widower for the second time, this time with five children between the ages of five and fourteen, Longfellow thought he might go mad with grief. Once, when earlier in their marriage he had attended a dance without Fanny, he reported, *"The lights seemed dimmer, the music sadder, the flowers fewer, and the women less fair."*

Now he was separated from her for eternity – or at least for the rest of his natural life. He told friends, "I am inwardly bleeding to death." So great was his grief, he feared he might be committed to an insane asylum.

In the end, it was his other two loves – his children and his writing – that saved him. He had to care for and provide for his children, so write he did.

Christoph Irmsher, in his *Longfellow Redux,* describes him as our "first and most successful celebrity poet." And he *was* a celebrity, earning a celebrity's income. At one point, he was receiving the equivalent of $80,000 *per poem.* If there had been such a thing as an American poet laureate at that time, he would have been it. His seventieth birthday was celebrated like a holiday nationwide. He received honorary degrees from Oxford and Cambridge, and was the first American to be honored with a bust in the Poet's Corner of Westminster Abbey. Schoolchildren routinely memorized his poems throughout the 1950s.

And his skills were not confined to writing poetry. Following his second wife's death, it was translations, in addition to poetry, that helped save him. He completed some of his most important works during this time, including translating Dante's *The Divine Comedy*.

Numerous other translations still stand as important contributions to our collective American literature. Early on, he published the 800-page *The Poets and Poetry of Europe*, which included not just his own translations but poems from other translators as well. Then, eight years before his death, Longfellow coordinated another ambitious project: the assembling of a 31-volume anthology called *Poems of Places*, comprised of poems from around the world. Although Emerson was critical of this undertaking as preventing Longfellow from writing more of his own original material, Longfellow's goal was always to introduce the general public to as many great poems as possible.

***

Longfellow could match Emerson quote-for-quote, and often expressed similar sentiments, although Longfellow's quotes often seem more personal and relatable than Emerson's lofty ones. A man or woman wounded by life can find a kindred spirit in the following:

There is no grief like the grief that does not speak.

They who go feel not the pain of parting; it is they who stay behind that suffer.

Every man has his secret sorrows which the world knows not; and oftentimes we call a man cold when he is only sad.

If we could read the secret history of our enemies, we should find in each man's life sorrow and suffering enough to disarm all hostility.

Fate was not kind to Longfellow in his personal life; history would be no kinder to his writing and reputation.

If the arc of Longfellow's talent and influence began in his teens and peaked in midlife, it ended shortly after his death. The bulk of Longfellow's works now reside between the covers of dusty books, rarely seeing the light of day anymore in elementary school classrooms or universities, dismissed as unoriginal and "children's poetry". Perhaps some can still quote "*Listen my children and you shall hear of the midnight ride of Paul Revere…*" and "*Under a spreading chestnut-tree, the village smithy stands…*" – but how many can recite more than that?

It was Emerson, not Longfellow, who enjoyed ongoing acclaim after his death. Emerson's works, like seeds carried in a pocket with a small hole, fell on fertile soil, took root, and spread. Historians point out that many of the important movements in the twentieth and even twenty-first century can be traced back to the thoughts and writings of

Emerson and the other members of his Transcendental Club.

These include civil rights, women's suffrage, environmentalism, simplicity and minimalism (all the rage now), and especially, America's spirit of rugged individualism: not a movement so much as an attitude, almost uniquely American.

Insist on yourself; never imitate...

Every great man is unique

None of us will ever accomplish anything excellent or commanding except when he listens to this whisper which is heard by him alone.

***

There are dangers inherent in each person's running around and acting according to the whisper heard by him or her alone. Certainly, much of modern relativism can be seen as flowing naturally from Emerson's emphasis on each individual deciding what is right and wrong.

In a society consisting of loosely connected individuals, an endless fracturing occurs. Reality sets in, for there will always be leaders and followers. As certain "self-actualized" individuals raise flags, others will fall in line behind them. This is certainly true in the realm of religion. In America, there are now more than 30,000 legally recognized Protestant and neo-Protestant denominations.

Harold Bloom has referred to Emerson as "the prophet of the American religion," which he describes as "Protestant but not Christian." He believes Emerson's thoughts and writings laid the groundwork for religious movements that started here in America, but then spread around the world. Two hundred years ago they didn't exist but today the Mormons, Christian Scientists, Seventh Day Adventists, Jehovah's Witnesses, and Scientologists have believers in almost every known country on the face of the planet, with followers numbered in the millions.

While not single-handedly responsible, but it does seem fair to lay many of these sects and upstart denominations at Emerson's doorstep.

CHAPTER 4

Joseph Smith (1805 – 1844)

As Emerson and Joseph Smith were contemporaries, it's natural to wonder how much the ideas of the former influenced the rise of the latter. Or maybe it was just the times in general. The embracing of new and unorthodox religious expression and the throwing off the shackles of traditional faith was rampant. Hang out a shingle, get a group to follow you, and soon you could be the leader of a new religious movement.

Joseph Smith did not become the leader of just any new religious movement. His Church of Jesus Christ of Latter-Day Saints, often referred to as Mormons, boasts more than 17 million adherents around the world and continues to be one of the fastest-growing religions in the world. Although they claim close kinship with Christianity, including belief in Jesus Christ as the Son of God, their non-Trinitarian view of the Godhead (three distinct persons) places them squarely outside traditional Christianity. So does the addition of the Book of Mormon as a sacred text.

Joseph Smith came from a religiously eclectic family. His mother was at least nominally Presbyterian while his father dabbled in Unitarianism, but mostly stayed away from church and followed his own ideas. Generations of the family, including parents, grandparents, aunts and uncles, were steeped in occult and mystical practices, including using "seer stones" for treasure hunting.

In September of 1821, Joseph Smith claimed he was led to a nearby hillside by an angel named Moroni. There he was shown golden tablets in an unknown language, describing an early history of a Christian civilization on the North American continent. Several years later, he was permitted to use his same "seer stone" to translate the golden tablets into the Book of Mormon. After the translation, the angel Moroni took the golden tablets back. Now seen as a prophet, Joseph Smith busied himself with building the faithful up into communities, constructing temples, and receiving new revelations.

Present-day Mormons follow strict prohibitions such as abstaining from alcohol and tobacco and even coffee and tea, and are also well-known for large but cohesive families and a strong work ethic. This was not always the case, as starting with the life of Joseph Smith, their communities were dogged by accusations of polygamous relationships. Smith and his wife, Emma, denied that he practiced polygamy but the evidence seems to clearly indicate otherwise; it was certainly true in the case of his successors, such as Brigham Young. A review of the likely 40 wives of Joseph Smith does indeed reveal a crazy quilt pattern of wives being "sealed" to Joseph Smith while married to their own husbands, a mother and daughter both married to Joseph Smith within a month of each other, and other connections quite scandalous to outside observers. For this reason, and others, they were often persecuted and driven out of communities until they finally settled in Utah.

Before that time, however, Joseph Smith and his brother, Hyrum, were shot and killed by a mob in Carthage, Illinois. The communities of true believers he had established were strong enough to flourish without their leader. Although there was some splintering into various groups, which remain today, the sect continues to thrive.

There is no denying that Joseph Smith, although largely uneducated, was a powerful and charismatic leader. When Smithsonian Magazine published its 2015 issue naming the 100 Most Significant Americans of All Time, ranked first in the category of religion is Joseph Smith, founder of the present-day Mormon church. Ranked third on the same list is Brigham Young, also a Mormon. Billy Graham didn't even make it into the Top Ten in the religion category.

How can this be? Some may wonder if the gauge of influence was based on sheer numbers. After all, Brigham Young had 55 wives, and 57 children by 16 of them. Even today, their birth rate is 25% higher than the national average and they now make up 7% of the population.

Surely the Smithsonian was looking at more than that.

In part, it may be that Mormons have recently enjoyed more acceptance into the mainstream, even fielding a presidential candidate when Mitt Romney headed up the Republican ticket in 2012. Other Mormons have served as state governors and influential political leaders in Washington, D.C., including Harry Reid's term as the

Democratic Speaker of the House from 2006 - 2012.

There is also the Mormons' keen sense of entrepreneurship. Examine any number of well-established companies and you will find they were formed by or are now run by Mormons. This includes companies like Jet Blue, Atari, Black and Decker, and Marriott.

In America, it's hard to argue with success.

Chapter 5

Esther Allen Howland
(1828 – 1904)

She was nineteen years old.

And a woman, living in Victorian times.

In 1847, Esther Howland had just completed her studies at Mount Holyoke Female Seminary (College), where she had been a classmate of Emily Dickinson. Stretched out before her lay the opportunities of…teacher or secretary, perhaps.

Stopping by her father's book and stationery store one day, she picked up a fancy English valentine left by a salesman. This was no mass-produced Hallmark card, but a delicate work of art trimmed in lace. Esther was captivated. An entrepreneurial spark fell among the dry dreams of previous months and burst into flame.

She set aside her diploma from Mount Holyoke in favor of a handful of things she hoped would prove more useful: her artistic talent, a strong work ethic combined with a natural knack for business and, important for the times, a family willing to support her and invest in her dreams.

Her father provided some of the necessary start-up supplies and she imported the rest from England. Gathering paper, paste, ribbon, and ink, she created her own versions of the English valentines. She wrote appropriately sentimental verses and had a brother with good handwriting copy them on the inside of the cards. Another brother was a traveling salesman for the family company.

Would he please take some of her samples on his next sales trip? Yes, he would. Just timidly beginning to believe in this dream of hers, Esther hoped he would return with $200 worth of orders.

He returned with $5000.

And thus, the woman who would become "The Mother of the American Valentine" took her first steps toward becoming New England's first independent businesswoman. She found a workspace and set up four friends in an assembly line along a long table. To the surprise of many, the orders continued to pour in. Over the next 34 years, Esther expanded her business and provided employment to a number of other women.

At no point were the cards mass-produced, for she never strayed from her original goal of making each card unique. The quality showed in the price—unusually high for the times. Many cards sold for $5 to $10 and elaborate ones with unusual lace and ribbons could sell for as much as $30 apiece. These were not valentines to be read and then tossed—these were works of art to wrap in tissue paper, place in a trunk, and pass down to future generations.

It is said some were used by shy young men to propose marriage!

Esther was described as a handsome woman, tall, with fine features and masses of dark chestnut hair. The only known picture shows her in her 50s, an unremarkable expression, looking heavy around the jowls. Although the masses of coiled chestnut hair are still visible, the picture no doubt doesn't do justice to her younger beauty.

This woman who devoted her life to creating declarations of love never married and the "Mother of the American Valentine" was never a mother herself. No matter. Her business was her baby, and she tended it as lovingly as any mother would her child.

In an era when women's artistic talents were largely confined to the drawing room in the forms of needlepoint, sketching, and watercolors, Esther Howland translated her artistic talent into a thriving business: The New England Valentine Company. The company eventually grossed $100,000 annually – nearly $3,000,000 in today's money.

Although she had brothers, her family provided her with opportunities outside the norm – not always a given in Victorian times. The support was expressed first by sending her to Mount Holyoke for higher education, then by her father supplying her with what she needed until her business got on its feet.

And it was *her* business. In addition to running the company, she remained involved in the hands-on artistic elements. She is credited with not just copying English valentines but improving on them, chiefly through her use of shadow boxes and brightly colored paper to highlight the lace. When a chronic knee problem confined her to a wheelchair in 1866, she still continued to oversee her business for the next fifteen years.

In 1881, Esther sold her New England Valentine Company

to George C. Whitney for a tidy sum, and retired to care for her elderly father. I imagine her sitting by her dying father's bedside and whispering, *"How do I love Thee? Let me count the ways…"* and then thanking him for all the times he believed in her, handing her the tools to follow her own dreams.

Over the course of her lifetime, Esther gained satisfaction both artistically and financially, rare for a woman in Victorian times when women married money or inherited money.

Esther earned her own money, and by doing what she loved.

Chapter 6

Jane Austin
(1831 – 1894)

No, not *that* Jane Austen. This author came along a century later, is American, not English, and spells her last name with an "i," not an "e." While our minds might immediately go to the fabulously popular British author, it's unlikely there was much confusion in this Jane Austin's lifetime, as the former's works did not become widely popular until the 20th century.

Jane was born Mary Jane Goodwin in Plymouth, Massachusetts. She was a prolific writer of poems, short stories, and novels. Her earliest writings, consisting mostly of poetry and short stories, were published in popular magazines of the times, including Harper's Monthly and The Atlantic.

During the second half of the 1800s, there was renewed interest in the story of the Pilgrims, especially in New England where Jane lived. Jane's father, who died when she was only two years old, had compiled many historical records related to the Pilgrims and done a great deal of genealogical research which proved Jane's family could trace their lineage to the Pilgrims through eight distinct lines. It's no wonder she chose to pivot her writing to capitalize on her family connections to and interest in the Mayflower passengers.

Today we would describe these writings as historical fiction, and it's evident she relied heavily on historical research. It was the fiction part that later scholars look askance at because several persistent myths about the Pilgrims can be traced back to her. Probably the most egregious one involves the wife of William Bradford, who served many years as the Governor of the Plymouth Colony.

After the Mayflower docked and a group of men hiked inland to discover food, water, and a place to build, many, including all of the women and children, remained on the ship for several months. The conditions were treacherous, as the Mayflower bobbed in ice-clogged waters and was buffeted by storms. When the men returned from their third scouting expedition, they learned that Dorothy Bradford had slipped on the icy deck and drowned. Jane decided to embellish the incident because she thought it made a better story to say she committed suicide because her husband was in love with one of the other women passengers. This is based solely on the fact that three years after being widowed, her husband did marry one of the other women passengers. It was a sparsely populated wilderness. Who else was he supposed to marry? This theme grew over time and the story later became that she committed suicide because of an unrequited love with the ship's captain, Christopher Jones. There is not a shred of evidence for either suicide theory, but still the myths persist.

Of course, Jane Austin is not the first Mayflower descendant to pen fanciful poetry or prose about the Pilgrims. Fellow John Howland descendant Henry Wadsworth Longfellow wrote the poem *The Courtship of Miles Standish* in 1858. In it, against the backdrop of a factual war with Native people, Longfellow concocted a story about a love triangle between Miles Standish, John Alden, and Priscilla Mullins. John Alden and Priscilla Mullins did marry in real life but there's no historical basis for the love triangle. Miles Standish was not a Separatist or "Saint" but one of the "Strangers," a military man hired to advise and protect the Pilgrims. Based on historical records that describe him as rather hot-headed and brutish, it's doubtful the demure and pious Priscilla would have found him a suitable match when the upstanding John Alden was available among her own kind. Nevertheless, *The Courtship of Miles Standish* was memorized and repeated by countless schoolchildren for decades, cementing it as part of our unquestioned Pilgrim mythology.

That's not to say that all of Austin's works about the Pilgrims and other early settlers are fanciful or lacking historical merit. Far from it. A number of her writings are still available and are regarded as important contributions to our modern understanding of life during those times, including *"Standish of Standish: A Story of the Pilgrims."* Despite her treatment of Dorothy Bradford, this book does not make up any love stories about Miles Standish and is regarded as historically accurate.

Other well-regarded historical fiction includes *Dr. LeBaron and His Daughters*, *The Tailor Boy*, *Dora Darling: The Daughter of the Revolution*, and *The Desmond Hundred*, the latter set in Ireland in the

1600s, against a backdrop of colonialism and oppression.

Those of us in northern climes who feel weary towards the end of winter, might relate to the hope expressed in one of Austin's early poems:

February

by Jane Goodwin Austin

I thought the world was cold in death;
The flowers, the birds, all life was gone,
For January's bitter breath
Had slain the bloom and hushed the song.

And still the earth is cold and white,
And mead and forest yet are bare;
But there's a something in the light
That says the germ of life is there.

Deep down within the frozen brook
I hear a murmur, faint and sweet,
And lo! the ice breaks as I look,
And living waters touch my feet.

Within the forest's leafless shade
I hear a spring-bird's hopeful lay:
O life to frozen death betrayed
Thy death shall end in life to-day.

And in my still heart's frozen cell
The pulses struggle to be free;
While sweet the bird sings, who can tell
But life may bloom again for thee!

CHAPTER 7

Phillips Brooks (1835 – 1893)

Just before the year 1000, Prince Vladimir of Kiev sent ten "wise envoys" out into the world to discover the best faith for his people. When they attended a liturgy in the magnificent cathedral *Hagia Sophia* in Constantinople, saw its beauty, and had their souls touched by the ethereal singing of the choir, they reportedly returned to the prince and told him, "We didn't know if we were in heaven or on earth; we only know that God dwells there among men." Thus began the Christianization of Russia in earnest.

Trinity Church in Copley Square, Boston, dedicated in 1877, has been called the American *Hagia Sophia*. It did not start out that way in location or structure, but what it became is largely due to a humble Episcopalian priest named Phillips Brooks.

Brooks was born in Boston and lived most of his life there. He graduated from Harvard at the age of twenty and, following his ordination as an Episcopal priest, served two churches in Pennsylvania before returning to Boston seven years later. By that time, he had developed a reputation as a powerful preacher and strong abolitionist. When he became rector of Trinity Church in 1869, he focused on serving his parishioners and reaching out to the surrounding area in active charity. For these reasons, his congregation soon outgrew its original building. In1872, they purchased a parcel of land on Copley Square.

Thus began his significant, although indirect, influence on American architecture.

It began when he reached out to a friend, architect H. H. Richardson, to design the new church. Not much is known about how they became connected, but their partnership on this project produced something brilliant. Brooks called the finished church "America's glory forever." A 2013 PBS special titled "Ten Buildings That Changed America" highlighted the impact of this single American church: not so much on the faith of America, as on its architectural legacy.

Richardson was only the second American formally trained in architecture but his earliest projects have been deemed "unremarkable." By the end of his relatively short career, however, (he died just 13 years after finishing Trinity Church), he was considered one of the "trinity" of American architects, along with Frank Lloyd Wright and Lloyd Sullivan.

But it was only H. H. Richardson of the three that had an architectural style named after him. His "Richardsonian Romanesque" spread west from Boston across much of the country where today many churches, libraries, post offices, train stations, and government buildings all bear the stamp of his architectural influence.

Prior to his magnificent work on Trinity Church, H. H. Richardson had designed only one other building featuring his signature style—the Buffalo State Asylum for the Insane. If the Reverend Phillips Brooks had not tapped him to design Trinity Church, would he have been discovered at all, or would he have died in obscurity? And how different would much of our American architecture from "sea to shining sea" look today?

***

One parishioner sitting in the pews at Trinity Church could not appreciate the beautiful stained-glass windows and striking murals by John La Farge, or hear the heavenly singing of the choirs. Did not, because she could not.

Young Helen Keller.

Her teacher, Annie Sullivan, brought her to Boston in 1888 to attend the Perkins School for the Blind. After sitting in church while having one of Brooks' powerful sermons translated for her, Helen exclaimed that she had "always known there was a God, but now I know his name." Brooks and Helen Keller corresponded until his death four years later. In his letters, he answered her questions and complimented her insights, above all else stressing God's love and care: *"And so, love is everything. And if anybody asks you, or if you ask yourself what God is, answer, 'God is Love.' That is the beautiful answer which the Bible gives."*

***

In addition to his parish duties, Brooks remained active on the campus of Harvard, his alma mater. He was very popular there, preaching in chapel and counseling the students. He turned down an offer of the Plummer Professorship of Christian Morals, however, fearing that his firm beliefs in Trinitarianism and the immortality of the soul would not be a good fit within the Unitarian atmosphere that dominated there. He had also received criticism for wanting to end compulsory chapel. Just as he wanted to free slaves physically, he said he wanted men's souls to *"be free to find the great Lord whom they ought to serve."*

Despite his full and hectic life, Brooks was reported to exhibit a genuine concern for all he met. He was also described as radiating a calm and serene demeanor at all times. When asked his secret, he shared: *"I am sure that it is a deeper knowledge and truer love of Christ...I cannot tell you how personal this grows to me. He is here. He knows me and I know Him. It is no figure of speech. It is the realest thing in the world. And every day makes it realer."*

As an indication of the high regard in which he was held by many and diverse groups within Boston, the whole city went into mourning when he died in January of 1893. Shops closed, the Boston Stock Exchange suspended business for the day, and more than ten thousand people crammed into Trinity Church and spilled out to fill all of Copley Square. A group of young students carried his casket from the Harvard campus to his resting place in Mt. Auburn Cemetery.

Rev. Brooks can still be found in the church, the university, and the city he loved. Statues of him stand inside and outside of Trinity Church, and at Harvard he appears in a stained-glass window in Memorial Hall. His name is engraved on the large wooden pulpit in Memorial Church and the Phillips Brooks House in Harvard Yard houses student-run volunteer groups.

For those who may never visit Boston, they can still experience his presence once a year at Christmas time. One Christmas Eve, remembering a trip to the Holy Land three years earlier, Brooks penned the words to the Christmas carol, "*O Little Town of Bethlehem*" and had his friend, organist Lewis Redner, set them to music. It still stands as one of the most tender and gentle of traditional carols.

Phillips Brooks was an immense man: 6'4" and 300 pounds. Although he projected a large presence, he was universally known for his humility. He once said, *"The true way to be humble is not to stoop until you are smaller than yourself, but to stand at your real height against some higher nature that will show you what the real smallness of your greatness is."*

For Brooks, this "higher nature" was found in the lowly manger.

CHAPTER 8

Florence Earle Nicholson Coates
(1850 – 1927)
Alice Nicholson Coates Trask
(1873 – 1955)

As a ninth-generation descendant of John Howland, Florence was one of twenty founding members of the SMDPA (Society of Mayflower Descendants in the Commonwealth of Pennsylvania), but she was certainly known for much more than that.

Born into privilege to a Philadelphia family, Florence Earle used her wealth, family background, and influence for a number of causes, including women's suffrage and civil rights for persons with disabilities. She came by this naturally. Her grandfather, Thomas Earle, was a prominent abolitionist and her father, George Earle, a lawyer who represented former slaves.

Florence was best known, however, as a prolific poet of nearly 300 original poems. Her family hosted the British literary critic and traveling lecturer, Matthew Arnold, when he was on an American tour. He encouraged her love of poetry and they became lifelong friends, with him serving as her mentor. She published frequently in literary magazines and journals such as Harper's, Lippincott's, Scribner's, The Century, The Literary Digest, and Atlantic Monthly. Her most famous poems reflected her love of the beauty of the Adirondacks, where her family had a summer home, and spiritual and patriotic themes. Her poetry was often set to music by well-known composers of the era. In 1915, Florence was elected the official poet laureate of the state of Pennsylvania.

If her professional life and activism for social causes both knew success, her personal life was touched by tragedy. In 1871, she married William Nicholson, who was deaf. He died just five years later. She was left with a young daughter, Alice, also deaf. In 1879, she married Edward Coates and although they enjoyed a successful marriage, their only child, another daughter, died in infancy.

Perhaps her daughter's deafness motivated her interest in securing civil rights for those with disabilities. In addition to her daughter's condition, she had a particular interest in and respect for Helen Keller. After viewing a photo of Helen Keller holding a rose, she was inspired to write a poem from Helen's perspective, excerpted below:

> *We understand each other, you and I!*
> *Thy velvet petals laid against my cheek,*
> *Thou feelest all the voiceless things I speak,*
> *And to my yearning makest mute reply;"*

In this interest, Florence was ahead of her time. It would be decades before a fellow John Howland descendant, George H. W. Bush, would pass the Americans with Disabilities Act in 1990.

Florence supported and encouraged her daughter, Alice, (a tenth-generation John Howland descendant), to become an accomplished person in her own right, despite her profound deafness. At a time when children with disabilities were often shut away, literally or figuratively, Alice became proficient in lip-reading, married, and founded two schools of lip-reading, one in Philadelphia and one in San Francisco. These schools were not residential schools but resources to help children with deafness go out into the world to succeed in whatever they chose to do. She served as the founder and president of the San Francisco League for the Hard of Hearing, taught classes, and published educational materials and scholarly works over a 20-year period. Having worked tirelessly to improve the lives of "the deafened," she died at the age of 82.

It's ironic that neither Florence's first husband nor her daughter ever heard from her own lips her beautiful poetry or the songs based on them, but through the power of her pen they were still able to be profoundly moved by reading them. Coates's poetry has stood the test of time; volumes of her poetry are still available today and her poetry is featured and discussed on current poetry blogs.

CHAPTER 9

Maude Adams (1880 – 1953)

Stage actress Maude Adams entered the world in Salt Lake City, Utah. Born to a Mormon mother, they didn't stay there long, for her mother was not the typical Mormon housewife of the late nineteenth century.

Acting was still considered morally suspect, but Annie Adams brought her daughter Maude on stage with her at the tender age of nine months. By age eighteen, Maude was a legitimate star, radiating genuine talent, as well as beauty. Her career spanned four decades, comprised of roles ranging from Shakespeare to characters created by James M. Barrie. At one point in her career, she was the highest paid stage actress of her time, earning more than one million dollars per year.

The title role in Barrie's Peter Pan is the one pixie-ish Maude Adams is most closely identified with. She once said, *"I had not finished the first act before the quaint character of Peter Pan had charmed me. I could feel the presence of the fairies and the Indians and the pirates and the lost boys of Never-Never Land."* She helped design the collar of her costume, which continues to be known even today as "the Peter Pan collar."

Maude was a study in contradictions. Ethel Barrymore described her as the original "I want to be alone" woman, yet she chose careers – acting and teaching – which placed her in the limelight. Although born a Mormon, she regularly retreated to Catholic convents for solitude and renewal.

The ultimate irony of her life? Being best known for playing the part of a young boy who refuses to grow up, yet herself growing into a woman with a combination of self-knowledge and self-discipline rare in her field.

She once wrote an essay titled, "The One I Knew the Least," where she described the challenges of discovering her own identity while spending her childhood assuming dozens of others. Her years with a "stage mother" did not send her spiraling out of control into drugs or drink, however. She chose contemplative retreats instead. She was fabulously wealthy, she refused to live a wealthy lifestyle. Instead, she used her wealth to support charities and to supplement the salaries of other actors.

And when she retired from the stage, she did not then lose her equilibrium either. She turned to teaching and served as head of the drama department for twelve years (1935-1947) at Stephens College in Missouri, where students loved her. She worked with General Electric to design better stage lighting, and holds three patents for lightbulbs. She also worked with the Eastman Company to develop color photography for film.

While teaching, Maude shared this philosophy with her students: *"Don't let anyone persuade you that anything we do in life less than our own best is a worthy thing. You must never compromise with your life. We know when we are doing first-rate things. When we satisfy ourselves with second-rate things, it is the beginning of a long, long death."*

Maude Adams never experienced that long, long death. Instead, she enjoyed the fruits of a long life, doing first-rate things. Earlier, she had donated her New York estate near Lake Ronkonkoma to the Catholic Sisters of the Cenacle. In death, she returned to join them there for her final rest.

Chapter 10

Edith Carow Roosevelt (1861 – 1948) and Her Children

The first John Howland descendant to live in the White House was not President Teddy Roosevelt, but Teddy's wife, Edith Carow Roosevelt.

Edith was Teddy's second wife; his first wife, Alice Hathaway Lee, died two days after giving birth to their daughter Alice Lee. Teddy Roosevelt's mother had just died twelve hours earlier, the same day, in the same house.

Teddy Roosevelt wrote in his diary that day: *"The light has gone out of my life."*

Overwhelmed by grief and disappointed by some of his political involvements, Teddy sought a new adventure to distract and entertain himself. He left his infant daughter with his beloved and capable older sister, Bamie (Anna) and headed to the Dakota Territory (now North

Dakota) to be a cattle rancher. After more disappointments when blizzards destroyed his herds, he gave up cowboy life and returned East. It was here he struck up a relationship with an old childhood playmate and former teenage sweetheart, Edith Carow.

Would Edith consider marrying him and becoming a stepmother to his young daughter?

Many a young woman might have hesitated to marry a man so overshadowed by tragedy, and especially because it was clear that he had never gotten over his first wife's death, his grief so profound that it was reported that he never mentioned her again, nor did he let anyone else speak her name in his presence. What must have been somewhat awkward, his daughter having the same name as his late wife, was solved by the family calling the girl "little Lee" (her middle name) for much of her early childhood.

And what of this little daughter? Even as a young child she had the reputation for being headstrong and spoiled. During his presidency, her father once said of his 17-year-old daughter, "I can run the country or I can attend to Alice, but I can't do both." Later in life, Alice described herself as a "hedonist," always out for a good time.

Then there was the prospective groom's personality to consider: definitely a macho male, restless and constantly seeking new adventures. A newspaperman once called him "an electric battery of inexhaustible energy."

Edith did agree to marry him but their wedding day of December 2, 1886, was not fortuitous. They married in London, England, and a thick, gloomy fog enveloped the church and surrounding area, causing some to think of it as an ominous omen.

Teddy's first wife was nicknamed "Sunshine" but when her "light went out of his life," Teddy found a second sun in Edith—brighter, stronger, and able to burn away the fog of previous misfortune.

During one part of their European honeymoon, Edith had only herself for company. Where was her new husband? Leading an expedition to the summit of Mt. Blanc in the French Alps, one of Europe's most deadly ascents. Later in life, desiring peaceful years with her husband following their hectic years in the White House, she instead gave her blessing to Teddy's big game safari in Africa and a year-long Amazon expedition sponsored by the Smithsonian that almost killed him.

She learned early not to tame him, just to love him.

When Edith and Teddy returned to America following their honeymoon, Teddy returned to involvement in politics. He is often pictured astride a rearing horse, waving a cowboy hat and shouting, "Bully!" but the image is too one-dimensional. The multi-faceted Teddy Roosevelt wore many hats throughout his life. He was a respected historian, author, explorer, soldier, and naturalist. As a politician, he is numbered by historians among the great American presidents. Along with Washington, Jefferson and Lincoln, his face is chiseled into Mt. Rushmore for posterity.

If behind every great man there is a great woman, in Teddy Roosevelt's case it was unquestionably Edith. He was proud of her as his intellectual equal. She was extremely well-read and he once described her as "not only cultured but scholarly." Because he trusted her judgment more than his own, she met with her husband every morning to advise him. She was his rock, and ark for the family he so dearly treasured. After once praising her many virtues to William Howard Taft, he concluded by saying, "She is closer to my ideal than I am myself."

In 1901, when Teddy Roosevelt became the twenty-sixth President of the United States following the assassination of President McKinley, the Roosevelt family had six children. The oldest was sixteen; the youngest three.

In the consensus of historians, Teddy Roosevelt is the father of the modern presidency. Equally true should be the acknowledgment of Edith as "mother" of the role of the modern First Lady. Because of their large brood, she spear-headed an extensive renovation and remodeling of the White House, which included the building of the West Wing to separate government offices from the family living quarters. Shortly thereafter, her husband dubbed their residence "The White House" and the name stuck.

After separating off a section for her family, Edith saw the remainder of the White House as a treasure for the American people and set about to make it as physically inviting and culturally important as possible. She expanded the State Dining Room. She hung portraits of the previous First Ladies in a special gallery and began the White House China Collection. She routinely entertained the wives of cabinet members and hosted musicales and other events. Whereas the previous First Lady, Ida McKinley, had been sickly and not very active in her role, Edith and Teddy were true partners in their life together in the new "White House."

There was one significant way in which they differed. Teddy enjoyed the attention of the press. His daughter Alice once remarked,

"My father wants to be the bride at every wedding, the corpse at every funeral, the baby at every baptism."

Edith, however, was less enamored of a gaggle of reporters hanging around the First Family. She had formal portraits taken of her family, which she passed out to the press corps in hopes they would try to take fewer photos of their own, but it didn't work. Reporters were naturally drawn to this large and lively presidential family and looked to them for entertaining headlines. There was usually no shortage.

Youngest son, Quentin, was a favorite with reporters because he was just so naughty. He often led the infamous "White House gang," which defaced presidential portraits with spitballs. He threw snowballs at security guards from the roof of the White House. Once he carved a ball field into the White House lawn—without permission, of course. Once he smuggled the family pony, Algonquin, into the White House and all the way up an elevator to his brother Archie's room to "cheer him up" during an illness. From Quentin up to rebellious teenager, Alice, it was quite the show for the nation.

"I don't think that any family has ever enjoyed the White House more than we have," President Roosevelt once remarked, and he gave the credit to his wife. How did she do it? By letting them be children during their childhoods and by letting them fill the White House with pets. Along with the pony and domesticated pets like cats and dogs, other household pets included snakes, badgers, raccoons, and a macaw named "Eli Yale." Edith understood her sons' needs so well that one of them once remarked, *"When Mother was little, she must have been a boy."*

What mother could ask for a better tribute?

Many years later, she also received a tribute from her stepdaughter, Alice, when Alice wrote in her autobiography, *Crowded Hours*, "That I was the child of another marriage was a simple fact and made a situation that had to be coped with, and Mother coped with it with a fairness and charm and intelligence which she has to a greater degree than almost anyone else I know."

There were royal battles between them during the teenage years, but it's to Alice's credit that she appreciated her stepmother down the road. Perhaps she was remembering with gratitude Edith's tireless hours of physical therapy with her after she contracted polio. As a result of her stepmother's hard work, which left them both in tears at times, Alice recovered without so much as a limp.

> *"One cannot bring up boys to be eagles and then expect them to be sparrows."*
>
> ~Edith Roosevelt, referring to her sons

But eagles and sparrows both fall from the sky. Before she died, Edith not only buried her husband, but three of her four sons—a pain no mother should have to know. Her youngest eaglet, Quentin, literally fell from the sky when he was shot down over France during World War I. He was only twenty; last born, but first to die.

During World War II, she lost her oldest, Ted Jr., one month after he led the invasion of Utah Beach on D-Day. A third, her sensitive Kermit, fell to the twin demons of alcohol and depression and took his own life.

In her later years, Edith filled her time with travel and writing, but also service. She spent many hours working with the Oyster Bay Needlework Guild, a charity that provided garments for the poor, and supported the work of social reformer Louis Riis, who worked to improve housing conditions for immigrants in crowded and rundown tenements. She once said, *"Nothing would please me more than when I die, they put this inscription on my tombstone: Everything she did was for the happiness of others."*

They did. They could also have added an inscription about courage in the face of grief.

In 1912, her husband was shot at close range while on the campaign trail. He unbuttoned his vest to show his blood-stained shirt, took bullet-riddled pages out of his pocket, and continued with his speech – for the next hour and a half. The bullet remained lodged in his chest for the rest of his life. When he finally died in his sleep in 1919, Vice President Marshall said, *"Death had to take him sleeping. If Roosevelt had been awake, there would have been a fight."* Son Archie telegrammed his siblings, *"The old lion is dead."*

When Edith died twenty-nine years later at the age of 87, her family lovingly laid her to rest next to the "old lion"— a lamb in terms of her placid demeanor, a lioness in terms of strength of character and her own accomplishments, including caring for her "cubs."

***

The Roosevelt children, also John Howland descendants:

Edith's oldest son, Theodore III (later known as Ted Jr.), shared all of his father's strength and vitality. He fought in both World Wars, although they were nearly thirty years apart.

In World War I, he suffered a gas attack and had his left kneecap blown apart. He came home, helped start the American Legion in 1919, and then began a series of appointments and accomplishments almost too numerous to list. He was an investment banker and businessman, serving as Chairman of the Board for American Express and Vice-President of Doubleday Books. He was a politician, serving as Governor of Puerto Rico and Governor-General of the Philippines. As Governor of Puerto Rico, his work on behalf of its citizens drew great praise. He taught himself Spanish so he could better understand and lead the people of Puerto Rico and raised funds among wealthy American philanthropists to build schools and improve the local economy.

He was both a Brigadier General in the US Army and Assistant Secretary of the Navy. He lived for the military exploits, which he loved; in the end, he died for them. In early 1944, Ted Roosevelt headed to England to help coordinate the Normandy invasion, although he was in his fifties and walked with a cane due to arthritis and previous war injuries like his blown-apart kneecap. He led his men in the first wave of troops to land by sea on Utah Beach—the only general to do so. When they realized they had arrived off course from their original objective, Roosevelt took over, modified the plans, directed tanks and troops inland to new positions, and was singularly instrumental in the success of the campaign. Years later, when General Omar Bradley was asked about bravery in combat, he listed Ted Jr's hobbling on a cane while coolly directing his men under enemy fire as the single bravest action he had ever observed. Ted Jr died one month later of a heart attack while still in Normandy and is buried there, next to his youngest brother Quentin, who was killed during World War I.

Second son, Kermit, and third son, Archie, were soldiers who, like their oldest brother, also fought in both World Wars. Archie has the distinction of being the only American ever classified as 100% medically disabled for the same wound incurred in two separate wars. His tombstone reads, "An old soldier, home from the war." Kermit, a skilled businessman and author, accompanied his father on demanding and dangerous trips to Africa and the Amazon.

And what of Ethel, the middle child with two older brothers, two younger brothers, and a glamorous half-sister always in the news? She chose not to compete for publicity, but she was just as beautiful—and just as strong. Her father once remarked that "she had a way of doing everything and managing everybody." This was not a criticism, but admiration, for she channeled her mother's efficiency and concern for others. Only ten when the family moved into the White House, before she left at seventeen her mother had routinely trusted her with White House duties like ordering food for dinners and assigning tasks to staff members.

Teddy Roosevelt had four sons when World War I broke out, but it was not one of his military-trained sons who first volunteered for service. It was his daughter, Ethel. Married to a surgeon sent to France to care for the wounded, Ethel traveled with him to work as a nurse in the Army Ambulance Hospital.

She saw tragedy up close, then had to face it herself. Like her mother, she suffered the pain of burying a child. Her firstborn and only son was so very young – only eight – when he died of septicemia. Her husband fell into a deep depression as a result and was unable to work for almost a decade. Ethel cared for him and their three little girls, keeping the family afloat until her husband recovered.

Later in life, she devoted countless hours to the civil rights movement and worked to bring low-income housing to Oyster Bay, New York. This caused a rift with some of her high society friends, but she persevered. The housing still stands. For sixty years, she volunteered with the Oyster Bay Red Cross. When it came time for her to sit for a formal portrait, she did not choose to wear a gown and pearls like other wealthy matrons.

She wore her Red Cross uniform.

Like mother, like daughter.

CHAPTER 11

Franklin Delano Roosevelt
(1882 – 1945)

Standing on the convention platform in Madison Square Garden, his weight distributed between his son's arm on one side and a crutch on the other, he eyed the podium a mere fifteen steps in front of him. He had no mobility in either leg, but an auditorium full of people sat expectantly awaiting his speech. His son carefully handed him the other crutch and held his breath as his father transferred his weight from him to it.

This had not always ended well in the past.

The crowd applauded at first, but then fell silent. Slowly, the man moved one crutch forward, leaned his weight onto it, and hitched the opposite leg up and forward before planting it on the ground and shifting his weight. Over and over he alternated the risky and painful gait until he reached the podium. His son sprang forward and grabbed the crutches as his father moved his brace-encased legs into position and clutched the sides of the podium with all his strength.

The floodlights magnified the beads of sweat glistening on his forehead.

A triumphant moment, but not a completely satisfactory one for the speaker, although he received thunderous applause at the end of his speech. *How much of it had been the result of pity or sympathy?* He wanted neither. After placing the name of his friend, Al Smith, into nomination as the 1924 Democratic candidate, Franklin Delano Roosevelt determined he would never again appear in public using crutches—the universal symbol of a cripple.

When FDR spoke at the 1928 Democratic convention four years later, he presented himself, in actions if not in words, as a "cured cripple." Indeed, he appeared to walk to the podium, still leaning on a son's arm but laughing and joking as he greeted guests – without a crutch in sight. In reality, however, he was anything but a cured cripple. The main thing that had changed was his extraordinary success at creating the *illusion* of no longer being crippled.

FDR once remarked to Orson Welles, "I believe you and I are the two greatest actors in America."

***

In Hugh Gregory Gallagher's splendid book, *FDR's Splendid Deception*, the author, a fellow wheelchair-bound "polio," makes the following startling observation: *"Franklin Delano Roosevelt was the only person in the recorded history of mankind who was chosen as a leader by his people even though he could not walk or stand without help."* It is truly a marvel that a man with complete lower paralysis could be elected to the presidency, a demanding job which involved constant travel, both domestic and foreign.

To say the life of a disabled person in the 1920s was grim is to utter an understatement. Many "cripples" died from kidney infections and pneumonia. Therapy barely existed. Equipment was cumbersome and painful. Unlike today, society provided no physical accommodations in buildings or public transportation. Many disabled citizens remained isolated at home or were shuttled off to institutions. Beyond the physical challenges, there existed the undisguised prejudice that the disabled were somehow morally and intellectually inferior. "Cripples" were often made fun of by comics.

As Hugh Gallagher points out, every person with paralyzed limbs has to think, at every moment, how to accomplish the simplest of tasks—how to dress, how to get to a bathroom, how to get in and out of buildings and vehicles, how to get from point A to point B. To all of this, FDR had to figure out how to do it all without even letting the disability show – and doing it while one of the most highly visible individuals of the twentieth century.

How on earth did he accomplish this?

FDR went to great lengths – literally – to conceal his disability. He had his tailor make extra-long pants to conceal his braces, the braces whose lower half he painted black to match his shoes. He had a metal bar added to his open-air touring car so he could pull himself to a standing position to greet the crowds. For hours on end, he practiced his "walking," where he leaned heavily on the arm of a companion and held a cane in a special way on the other side so that it served as a crutch in usefulness, but didn't look like one.

Still a strong and vigorous man from the waist up, FDR labored to keep all the attention above his belt. He cultivated an image of a jovial, almost carefree individual, his chin high in the air, a big grin, a long cigarette holder clamped in his teeth at a jaunty angle, his fedora—all part of the image he worked hard to project.

His hard work paid off. Technically, everyone knew the president was crippled but there existed so little visible evidence, many seemed to forget. Political cartoons never once showed him in a wheelchair or even in braces, but instead, often as running or jumping. It helped that he held office before the advent of television but even so, an ever-present gaggle of reporters and photographers followed him. Of the more than thirty-five thousand (35,000!) photos they snapped during his time in office, only two show him seated in a wheelchair.

And these were never seen by the general public.

The wheelchair and braces were the least of what the public didn't see. Behind the scenes, FDR paid a great physical and emotional price to maintain his illusion. In several instances, to disguise his disability, FDR had assistants carry him up an outdoor fire escape at the rear of the building. Once, when the fire escape was only wide enough for one person, FDR sat down backwards and dragged himself up the fire escape by his arms, one step at a time, until someone met him at the top. After wiping the sweat from his face and straightening his clothes, he was transported to a normal chair, not a wheelchair, and delivered his speech.

No, polio did not end his political career, as well it might have in that era. Neither did another common political career-killer: an extra-marital affair. Oddly enough, these two – a crippling disease and infidelity – combined to propel FDR's political career to unimagined heights.

***

In the summer of 1921, Franklin Delano Roosevelt gathered his family and headed to Canada's Campobello Island, a favorite vacation spot. On August10, he and his three oldest children discovered a forest fire on another island. It was a great game, but also exhausting, to beat it out with pine branches over the course of several hours. To clean up and refresh, they jogged two miles to swim in a lagoon, followed by a swim in the bay.

Normally FDR, not yet forty, would not have batted an eyelash at this level of activity. This day, however, he could not shake his exhaustion, so he retired upstairs for a nap.

He woke up from that nap as a different person.

Over the next several days, he became completely paralyzed from the chest down and experienced fever and unbearable pain throughout his body. The paralysis eventually retreated until only his lower limbs were affected, giving him hope that he would one day conquer the paralysis completely.

Years before this illness, FDR had outlined his ambitions: serve in the New York Assembly, be appointed Assistant Secretary of the Navy, get elected as governor of New York…and then on to the White House. When polio struck, he had already served three years in the New York State Senate and as Assistant Secretary of the Navy. He was right on track for his ultimate goal.

His mother now wanted him to retreat to the family home in Hyde Park, New York, to live the life of a semi-retired invalid. She could bankroll this lifestyle, and would have happily done so.

Eleanor wanted him to continue with his original political goals.

While Roosevelt did retreat from public life for most of the next seven years, it was not to live the life of a semi-retired invalid on his mother's estate at Hyde Park, although he did spend a good deal of time there during the early years of his illness. His retreat from public life was for the purpose of pursuing any and all possibilities for regaining his mobility.

Years later, when FDR told the American people that they needed to *"Do something. If it works, do more of it. If it doesn't, do something else,"* he was speaking from his personal experience. Throughout his lifetime, FDR refused to accept the doctors' verdict that he would never walk again. In the beginning, he chased every possible cure, no matter how far-fetched. Although he never found a cure, in chasing one he did stumble across an oasis that would come to consume much of his time and a good part of his personal fortune. If not for the influence of his wife, Eleanor, it might have become his life's work.

In 1924, FDR visited Warm Springs, Georgia, and was encouraged by the way his body responded to exercising in the highly mineralized, eighty-eight-degree pure spring water that flowed from Pine Mountain. In 1926, he bought the decrepit Meriwether Inn and surrounding property in Warm Springs and designed a rehabilitation facility to care for polio victims. He expanded and upgraded buildings and designed rehabilitation programs that included surgery, strengthening exercises, and mobility training. More than caring for polio victims, it became a center for research. He was known there as "Dr. Roosevelt" and he loved it.

But where was his wife, Eleanor?

A decade earlier, Eleanor had been unpacking her husband's suitcase after a trip when she discovered a packet of love letters. The letters left no doubt that an ongoing affair existed between her husband and her social secretary, Lucy Mercer. History will forever debate whether it was a physical affair or merely an "affair of the heart," but nevertheless, Eleanor was devastated and offered her husband a divorce. FDR might well have accepted, despite its effect on his political ambitions, had his mother not intervened. Sara Delano Roosevelt made clear the dire consequences of a divorce, not the least of which included an end to her generous financial support. So FDR told Lucy rather disingenuously that Eleanor would not consent to divorce, and he and Eleanor formed an "armed truce" (in their son's words) which allowed Eleanor great freedom to pursue her own independent goals, most of them political.

Little did FDR realize at the time that the affair would wind up helping his career, instead of hurting it.

Without the discovery of the affair, Eleanor would have loyally devoted herself to his long rehabilitation. As it was, feeling humiliated and heartbroken, as well as tired of being under the thumb of her domineering mother-in-law, Eleanor determined to throw herself into her own work. In the end, she proved to be her husband's greatest political asset.

FDR did not totally abandon his political career during the seven years he stepped back from public life, for he kept up a steady correspondence with political allies and found ways to win favorable publicity. But overall, it was his therapy and rehabilitation center in Warm Springs that absorbed the majority of his attention – and money.

Back in New York, Eleanor and FDR's friend and political advisor, Louis Howe, continued their active political work on FDR's behalf. They kept his name in front of important political leaders; they attended and spoke at rallies and conventions in his place. Eleanor became highly involved in Democratic politics at both the state and national level, pursuing interests that meant the most to her, but always with a thought about how to advance her husband's political career.

While FDR never doubted he would walk again, Eleanor never doubted he could achieve his original political goals, even if he never walked again.

In 1928, Al Smith, the Democrat presidential hopeful, badly wanted FDR to run for governor of New York to help his own ticket. He tried everything to convince FDR, from donations to his rehab center to reassurances that FDR could do minimal campaigning and an able lieutenant governor would attend to the actual day-to-day governing, leaving FDR free to spend as much time as he wanted at Warm Springs. FDR remained resolutely against the idea, as he felt morally bound to continue his work in Warm Springs, having invested so much money and with so many people counting on him.

Eleanor then entered the fray. Instead of sharing her concern that he was burying himself and his career in rural Georgia, she stressed that this was the next step he himself had always planned for on his journey to the White House. Finally, FDR conceded that while they did not have his permission to place his name for the nomination, if elected by acclaim, he would accept.

He was, and he did.

In the actual election, FDR won by one-half of one percent – the only Democratic win in a Republican sweep that year – but he was back on track.

Three years later, he accepted his party's nomination as their presidential candidate for 1932, jumping into that race with both feet – completely hidden from view. Nine days after accepting the nomination, he rented a boat with three of his sons and, with a host of reporters, sailed up the coast to New England. There wasn't a wheelchair, crutch or brace in sight, at least not as recorded by the reporters. Instead, the American public saw a vital, vigorous, and charismatic candidate ready to tackle the nation's crushing problems.

The rest, as they say, is history.

***

Years later, Eleanor was to describe her husband's polio as "perhaps a blessing in disguise."

Why?

First of all, the experience transformed this man so frequently described as a "lightweight" in his younger years. His paralysis forced him to develop patience and persistence where previously, good things had flowed effortlessly into his life.

Secondly, because of his privileged and sheltered upbringing, his disability now exposed him to a world of challenges and suffering never before seen by him. Warm Springs, Georgia, was a completely new world to him, a world where he was constantly forced to interact with the "common man." Not forced, exactly, for he was naturally gregarious. He had a Model T fitted with hand controls and often took the car out into the countryside surrounding the rehabilitation center, where he stopped and talked to people along the way. More important than talking, he listened. He heard their concerns, and saw their poverty.

Together with Eleanor's blossoming commitment to the poor and disadvantaged, they would make a formidable political team.

***

After a decade of dealing with a devastating physical disability, FDR approached the 1932 election with a commitment to, in his own words, *"...bold, persistent experimentation"* and a sense of strength, confidence, and hope. He told his fellow citizens: *"The country needs, and unless I mistake its temper, the country demands, bold, persistent experimentation. It is common sense to take a method and try it; if it fails, admit it frankly and try another. But above all, try something."*

FDR did try something, and tried it right away. Following his inauguration on March 4, he "marched forth" to do battle against the banking crisis. He declared a banking "holiday" to halt bank runs while he worked on a fix. On March 9, he called a special of session of Congress and presented a bill to stabilize failing banks, which Congress passed that same day. On March 12, he held his first "fireside chat" over the radio. On March 13, he reopened the reorganized banks and Americans, expressing faith in their new leader, began once more to deposit more than they withdrew.

Crisis averted. In just ten days.

Over the first one hundred days, Roosevelt spearheaded an unprecedented amount of legislation: a total of fifteen bills passed between March and mid-June. The new legislation touched on everything from banking to Prohibition, from farm commodities to collective bargaining.

The Civilian Conservation Corps planted trees and fought forest fires. The Tennessee Valley Authority Act built dams to control flooding and provide affordable energy in an impoverished region. The Public Works Administration (PWA) oversaw a significant investment in the country's infrastructure. Through private construction contracts, many large-scale public works took shape, providing national and local pride along with employment. With an investment of more than six billion dollars, private contractors built bridges, tunnels, highways, airports, hospitals, and government buildings, more than 34,000 projects between 1933 and 1939. It is estimated that every year PWA projects consumed half of the concrete and a third of the steel being used across the nation. Many of the projects remain today, including the Grand Coulee Dam in Washington state and the Fort Peck Dam in Montana (one of the largest in the world), the causeway that connects Key West to the Florida mainland, and in New York City, both the Lincoln Tunnel and parts of LaGuardia International Airport.

In spite of all this, two years into FDR's first term the economy still limped along, so FDR continued experimenting and "doing things." In the spring of 1935, he initiated an aggressive second-round of government programs which expanded the original New Deal. With this, the New Deal became a "big deal"– touching nearly every aspect of the economy and American culture.

Unlike the PWA, the Works Progress Administration (WPA), begun in 1935, concentrated on smaller projects and directly hired the unemployed. Workers drained swamps to combat malaria. Children brought their shoes to school to be repaired by a WPA-financed shoe repairman. Librarians traveled by horseback deep into isolated rural areas to bring books otherwise inaccessible. There were projects for artists, writers, and actors.

In August of 1935, the Social Security Act (SSA) provided for a formalized system of federal pensions, and Aid to Dependent Children, part of the Social Security Act, laid the groundwork for the modern welfare system. In living out his vision of a paternalistic government, he created federal programs that he thought a good father ought to do: provide for your welfare. In so doing, he forever reshaped the relationship between the government and the people of the United States.

Love him or hate him for his massive expansion of the federal government, things would never be the same after his presidency.

***

FDR did not in fact lead the United States out of the Great Depression. High unemployment rates remained clear through 1941 and many of the jobs he created through his "alphabet soup" programs and agencies were short-term, stop-gap measures without lasting value. World War II provided a temporary boost to the economy but as the war wound down, Roosevelt felt panicked at the thought of all the soldiers returning home and looking for work. Coupled with the millions of citizens who would lose their war-related jobs, he feared a return of high unemployment and what that might trigger. With the end of the war on the horizon, he quickly began to prepare a "New Deal revival."

Surprisingly, Roosevelt's Democrat-controlled Congress said "no" to these plans. Perhaps they understood that a number of the original New Deal programs had not worked quite as well as originally thought. Instead, a round of tax cuts led to investments in businesses that gave the economy the sustainable boost it needed.

What Roosevelt did do was lead America *through* the Great Depression. He did it by becoming, long before Ronald Reagan, the "Great Communicator," his strong and decisive yet soothing and fatherly voice traveling over the airwaves and into the living rooms of average families across the country. During his three-plus presidential terms, FDR spoke directly to his fellow citizens in a total of thirty of these fireside chats. These were not "press conferences," but something far more innovative and effective.

And those stop-gap jobs he created? Perhaps they did not bring the country out of the Great Depression, but in the short term, they were all that stood between starvation and survival for many poor families. They provided self-esteem when badly needed. Instead of holding out a hand to collect a government check, the unemployed jumped at the chance to use their hands to accomplish things, useful things they and their neighbors could see and feel good about. These short-term jobs created a needed stability for individuals, families, and the nation.

FDR's biggest contribution to the country may not have been any particular program, but the intangibles that held the nation together: Strength. Confidence. Hope.

***

As FDR navigated the United States through the domestic minefield of the Great Depression, an international crisis was looming: World War II in Europe.

If he has perhaps been given too much credit for resolving the Great Depression, a recent book by Nigel Hamilton makes the case that he has received too little credit for guiding the victories of World War II. In *The Mantle of Command: FDR at War 1941 – 1945*, the author sheds new light on FDR's hands-on approach to guiding the military strategy of the war.

The title of Commander in Chief was not a ceremonial one for FDR. According to Hamilton, FDR had no problem overruling his own military advisors and field commanders. He vetoed an invasion across the English Channel, strongly recommended by his Joint Chiefs of Staff, US Army Chief of Staff George Marshall, and Secretary of War Henry Stimson. Instead, he threw his weight behind "Operation Torch," the ultimately successful campaign in northern Africa that many credit as one of the significant turning points of the war.

In the Pacific, Hamilton claims that it was also FDR who ordered the Tokyo or "Doolittle" Raid – the first air raid attack on the Japanese mainland – and directed the Battle of Midway, one of the most decisive naval battles in the region, if not the war.

Shortly after the attack on Pearl Harbor in December 1941, Churchill flew to the White House to celebrate Christmas with FDR. During the course of the war, the two men formed a deep and abiding friendship, even when they failed at times to agree on certain points, natural enough when each ultimately had responsibility for his own country's best interests. During the war-torn years, they met an unprecedented eleven times in person and exchanged nearly two thousand written communications. FDR ended one letter to Churchill by saying, "It's fun to be in the same decade with you."

He might well have added, "It's fun to be in the same *family* with you" for while FDR was descended from John Howland, Winston Churchill was descended from John Howland's brother, Arthur.

***

When FDR picked up the mantle of command to deal with domestic and international crises, he never removed the mantle of command he had assumed in the battle against polio. As president, he found a broader platform from which to drum up support. On January 30, 1934, a series of balls were held across the nation to celebrate the new president's birthday. FDR determined this would be a great opportunity to make an appeal for his favorite charity. Although in the depths of the Great Depression, organizers raised one million dollars that first year. He held these balls annually for the rest of his tenure as president, generating ongoing funding in the fight against polio.

In 1937, FDR created the non-partisan National Foundation for Infantile Paralysis to better organize treatment and fund polio research.

While Roosevelt was certainly experienced at creating government programs, he envisioned this one being funded entirely by donations.

But how could he ask citizens deep in the Great Depression to give anything more?

A popular entertainer at the time, Eddie Cantor, suggested they make an appeal for "just a dime at a time" and call it "The March of Dimes," a takeoff on the American radio news series broadcasts called "The March of Time." At the president's request, postcards with dimes taped to them came pouring in. Although polio has been all but eliminated today, the March of Dimes continues, now focusing its work on preventing premature births and birth defects, and supporting families of newborns receiving neonatal care.

Through FDR's unfailing dedication to fund raising and research, he turned the tide against an illness that had plagued humanity for centuries, for evidence of polio dates back to the Egyptian mummies. Although Eleanor didn't know it at the time, perhaps this was also part of FDR's polio being "a blessing in disguise."

FDR died on April 12, 1945. Exactly one decade later, on April 12, 1955, the foundation he organized announced the success of Jonas Salk's polio vaccine. Today, polio cases around the globe number fewer than twenty in any given year.

Its complete eradication is within humanity's reach.

It took fifty-two years before a memorial to FDR was built in Washington, DC but just nine months after his death – on what would have been his 64th birthday – the United States mint issued a dime with FDR's likeness on it. There it has remained for the past seven decades. Nearly every American has, at one time or another, held a dime in their hand and felt between their fingers the profile of FDR, a man who fought three battles – the Great Depression, World War II, and the war on polio – and prevailed in all three.

Although the dime is the thinnest American coin, it bears the likeness of a man whose influence on the nation, and the world, was anything but slim.

CHAPTER 12

Ruth Wales du Pont
(1889 – 1967)

Not everyone was a fan of the new Roosevelt dime, but we'll get to that later…

As recently as 2014, decades after her death, composer Brian Cox described Ruth Wales du Pont as a "significant but forgotten composer." The fact that she was a composer at all is remarkable in that she didn't begin taking piano lessons until she was 13. And yet, during her lifetime, she composed pieces as varied as a ragtime chorus to opera, some of which are still being performed.

Ruth was born in Hyde Park, a wealthy New York suburb, but her family wealth was not consistently stable. Her father was frequently absent, chasing schemes and skirts in Washington, DC. She was raised by her mother and maternal grandmother, with infrequent visits from her father. Both sides of the family had some wealth and prominence and as a teen, Ruth attended Miss Spence's, a private boarding school.

She participated in and enjoyed the upper-class social scene, especially in Southampton on Long Island, where her paternal grandfather had a large summer home known as "Ox Pasture"; not a very romantic name, but apparently quite lovely, just the same.

It was after her family rented a home in Washington DC, where her paternal uncle by marriage was a prominent politician, that Ruth entered a new upper class social scene in which she was often thrown together with Henry "Harry" Francis du Pont, the son of a former US Senator and colonel.

Harry and Ruth were a perfect illustration of the maxim "opposites attract." Ruth was beautiful and vivacious, interested in parties and the arts; Harry was shy and introverted, interested in horticulture and antiques. To her credit, Ruth saw beyond Harry's shy exterior to the interesting, kind, and sensitive man beneath. At the end of a seven-year, somewhat uneven courtship, Ruth and Harry wed in 1916. She was an only child marrying an only child. Despite many privileges, both had had somewhat difficult childhoods. Harry was the only one of his parents' six children to live and thus suffered the twin challenges of a mother who coddled him and a father who was strict and demanding. And yet, by all accounts, as revealed through written letters and anecdotes by those who knew them, Ruth and Harry were able to forge a strong marriage where, as a devoted couple, they remained much in love throughout their 50 years together.

Whether or not composer Brian Cox is correct that Ruth du Pont deserves more credit for her classical compositions, one contribution to American culture associated with Ruth has endured, and that is the establishment of Winterthur Museum, Gardens and Library.

Ruth and Harry had spent much of the first decade of their marriage at Winterthur (pronounced "winter-tour"), the du Pont's family estate near Wilmington, Delaware. It was a challenging decade. Harry's doting mother was deceased so Harry's tyrannical father ruled the roost. So challenging was his rule that at one point Ruth spent three weeks at Austen Riggs Hospital for her "nerves." When the senior du Pont died in 1926, Harry and Ruth were freed to be the team they were meant to be. Harry's full inheritance of the estate allowed him to fulfill his dream of turning Winterthur into a large museum of Americana, along with vast gardens.

Harry's interest in horticulture and agriculture began in his childhood and continued throughout his life. On their three-month honeymoon across the North American continent, Harry busily gathered seeds and plants to expand his already impressive gardens. Over the years, Winterthur's 175-room mansion has grown to encompass the largest collection of American furniture (9,000 pieces) in the world, dating from the mid-1600s to the mid-1800s. It also includes nearly 90,000 objects of diverse American decorative arts, including textiles, glass, ceramic, woodworking, and metalwork. It is considered the largest and finest collection of Americana anywhere in the world.

Until the death of Harry du Pont in 1969, the grounds used to boast an extensive farm where, among other livestock, he raised a prize-winning herd of Holstein-Friesian cattle. The museum and now the library (100,000+ volumes, including 20,000 rare American and European editions) sits on 1,000 acres of massive gardens, as well as fields and wetlands, streams, grassy paths, and woodlands. It is visited by an average of 100,000 people every year.

The du Ponts' collections, although amassed by a wealthy family, were not kept as private collections. As early as 1951, they were opened to the public to be shared by all Americans, to foster an appreciation of their culture. Ruth's contribution to this American gem may be more indirect but no less important. While she did play the grand piano at Winterthur to entertain guests, her most important contribution to the project was the unfailing love and support she provided to its founder, her husband.

Yet, despite this and her many other fine qualities, talents, and contributions, Ruth was regrettably a little too aware of and committed to class distinctions. She was a neighbor and friend of Franklin Delano Roosevelt during her childhood in Hyde Park. Roosevelt was also a classmate of her husband at Groton, and was a guest at their wedding. The friendship not only did not endure but actually became quite sour, at least on Ruth's part.

There is no evidence that FDR felt any antipathy towards Ruth but for Ruth, a staunch Republican, FDR's New Deal policies caused an irreparable break, as she felt he had "betrayed his class." Perhaps she read the following FDR quote and thought it hit a little too close to home: "No government can help the destinies of people who insist on putting sectional and class consciousness ahead of general weal."

There is also no evidence that either realized they were actually (quite) distant cousins, each a descendant of John and Elizabeth Howland. If they did know this, the family connection was apparently not enough to overcome political differences. So strong were Ruth's feelings that she actually wrote to the Secretary of the Treasury in 1954 to demand that they stop minting Roosevelt dimes. Not only that, she wanted them to recall all of the ones currently in circulation, stating she herself would pay for it! (It didn't happen.)

Chapter 13

Dr. Benjamin Spock (1903 – 1998)

Time Magazine called his simple little book "one of the most revolutionary books in American history."

What was it? Something by one of the Founding Fathers? Something connected to the American Revolution?

No, it was Dr. Benjamin Spock's Common Sense Book of Baby and Child Care, first published in 1946. It originally sold for just 25 cents per copy. It is now in its 10th edition.

"Children should be seen and not heard" guided parents for generations. In many well-to-do families, children were essentially raised by nannies and had few deep emotional ties with their parents. In poorer families, children were seen as cheap labor, both inside and outside of the house.

Children were primarily expected to be respectful and industrious. To aid in this, experts instructed parents to follow rigid schedules with their children, and warned against too much physical affection. Time for bed? A child might get a kiss on the forehead. Might. Your child just excelled in school or sports? A hearty clap on the shoulder should suffice. Dr. John Watson, in his 1928 book "Psychological Care of Infant and Child," actually gave the following advice: "Never, never kiss your child." For good measure, he added, "Never hold it in your lap. Never rock its carriage." Its? Yikes!

To be sure, not every parent had the self-restraint to keep from scooping up their bundles of joy and smothering them with kisses, although that was more often the domain of grandmothers and maiden aunts, and usually confined to infants and toddlers. Until the advent of Dr. Spock, most parents still believed that too much affection would spoil their children for the rigors of the real world.

Spock was the oldest of six children and says he received a good deal of experience with and insight into children from helping to raise his five younger siblings. He received his undergraduate degree from Yale and graduated first in his class from Columbia University's College of Physicians and Surgeons in 1929, with a specialty in pediatrics. He was also part of an Olympic rowing team that won a gold medal at the 1924 Olympics in Paris.

When World War II came along, it shook a lot of things up. "Rosie the Riveter" had flexed her muscles, literally and figuratively. When World War II ended, soldiers flocked home, ready to settle down, marry, raise their families, and enjoy the fruits of America's new booming post-war economy. The economy wasn't the only thing booming. The "Baby Boom" was underway, but as women returned in droves to the more traditional roles of full-time mother and homemaker, it was to a different hearth, and a different home, from those of their mothers and grandmothers.

Throughout the 30s and early 40s, Dr. Spock had been studying psychoanalysis. He said he realized early in his practice that parents had as many questions about their child's psychosocial development as they did about their child's physical development. Not unlike Carl Rogers' person-centered therapy, Spock set about to design a more child-centered type of baby and child care.

He took his time and tried out some of his new ideas in his own practice. He listened to mothers' questions and their input. He later stated: "I learned it all from the mothers." In 1946, just in time for the end of the war and the evolving new post-war era, he felt ready to publish what he had learned.

In his obituary, Time magazine claimed Spock "almost single-handedly revolutionized the way parents interacted with their children." A fairly strong claim.

Just what was so revolutionary about this book?

The heart of his philosophy was contained in the title of the first chapter: "Trust Yourself." This was followed by the opening line of the first paragraph: "You know more than you think you do." When this new generation of mothers heard his basic message, they embraced it and couldn't turn the pages fast enough.

What, beyond the opening line, was so remarkable?

First, it covered a range of topics, not just a child's physical needs.

Second, there was his tone. Instead of the wise expert imparting wisdom, Spock wrote in a down-to-earth, conversational manner.

Third was the advice itself, so different from what parents had heard before. Spock presented children as little people with their own needs, including psychological needs, rather than lumps of clay to be molded into model citizens.

Out with rigid schedules; in with listening, and hugging, and flexibility.

The book was an instant success, selling half a million copies in its first six months. Over the next fifty years, only the Bible outsold it. Today, over seventy years later – amid a wealth of parenting advice available online, in other books, and in parenting magazines – Spock's book continues to sell. It has been translated into fifty different languages.

Spock introduced the concept that parents generally know what's best for their own children. In fact, he once boldly stated, "The more people have studied different methods of bringing up children, the more they have come to the conclusion that what good mothers and fathers instinctively feel like doing for their babies is the best after all."

It might seem odd to us now that this was ever questioned – but it was.

Spock was our first "celebrity" pediatrician, with his own TV program and newspaper column. His reputation took a hit during the Sixties, however, when the term "Spock Baby" took on a negative meaning. The "spoiled and lazy" younger generation of the 1960s was thought to be the result of Spock's coddling and too much instant gratification. He didn't help his cause when he threw himself headlong into the Sixties, joining Vietnam protests and supporting left-wing causes. The 'father' (or perhaps 'grandfather') of several generations of babies became a child of the times when he left his wife after forty-eight years of marriage, married a woman forty years his junior, became a vegan, took up yoga and meditation, and involved himself in government protests. For the final decades of his life, he became known as the "father of permissiveness," but he defended himself by saying, "I never wanted to encourage permissiveness, but rather to relax rigidity."

He also received criticism for recommending a sleeping position for infants that was later tied to SIDS, and for recommending vegan diets for children over the age of two.

But much of the value of his advice remains. He stressed that parenting should be fun and that fathers should be actively involved in child rearing. Ahead of his time, he even identified postpartum depression, what he called "the blues."

And tonight, as millions of parents put their children to bed after cuddling and kissing them and telling them that they are special and precious, they may have Dr. Benjamin Spock to thank for his encouragement to do so.

Chapter 14

Eville Gorham
(1925 – 2020)

Not all of John Howland's descendants who went on to make important contributions to society were, or are, native-born Americans. Such is the case of Canadian-born Eville Gorham, the impact of whose scientist research changed the world. Many consider him the "grandfather of acid rain research." As early as the 1950s, he began to sound the alarm about the negative effects of acid rain being linked to the burning of fossil fuels.

"I never set out to save the environment," he once said, but that's what his life's work soon became.

Eville Gorham was born in Halifax, Nova Scotia, where he immersed himself in the natural world around him. Although the majority of his later research occurred in England and his teaching and environmental activism took place in the United States, it was his experiences during his rural Canadian childhood that first shaped him.

After receiving his undergraduate degrees in Biology and Zoology in Halifax, he set off for England to add a PhD in botany. Following a post-doctoral project involving peatlands in Sweden, he returned to England to settle in the Lake District there to focus on *limnology*, the physical study of inland waters and their biological and chemical interaction with their environments. He concentrated mostly on peatlands, bogs, and inland lakes.

By studying both rain blown in from the sea (which was polluted) and rain blown in from industrial areas (which was also polluted), he was able to demonstrate the insidious effects of air pollution on ecosystems far from the original source of the pollution. This led to detailed studies about the results of acid rain. He then moved on to study the effects of air pollution on humans, laying the groundwork for future environmental activism.

Researching radiation from nuclear fallout was a related study with far-reaching results. Through his own study of radiation levels in sphagnum moss, combined with others' researching radiation levels in lichen in northern climes, the eyes of the scientific world were opened to the far-reaching, even global consequences, of fallout from nuclear testing. This helped lay the groundwork for the Atmospheric Nuclear Test Ban of 1963.

His research also led to environmental legislation and designs for cleaner power plants.

After a five-year stint back in Canada, Eville accepted a teaching job at the University of Minnesota, where he remained for the rest of his career. He focused his time on teaching, environmental projects, and activism. Gorham testified before Congress and was appointed to the White House Council on Environmental Quality. During his lifetime, he served on numerous American and international environmental committees, commissions, and projects.

It's difficult to overstate how much his research over a 60-year period contributed to our present understanding of environmental concerns.

Eville died at the age of 94 in January, 2020, just weeks before the outbreak of the Covid pandemic.

Chapter 15

George H. W. Bush (1924 – 2018)

At nineteen, George Bush, Sr. became the youngest-ever Navy pilot of a torpedo bomber. The next year, 1944, he piloted one of four aircraft undertaking a raid near Chichi Jima, a small island south of Tokyo. Not unlike his ancestor, John Howland, he experienced a miraculous escape.

A dozen "Flyboys" took off on the mission.

Only one returned.

Emerson once said, *"A hero is no braver than an ordinary man, but he is brave five minutes longer."* Bush was brave those extra five minutes. With his engine on fire, he told his two crewmates to bail, then continued the mission, dropped his bombs on the intended target, and flew several miles farther before parachuting out. He hit his head on the plane's tail, incurring a head wound, but survived. Several hours later, he was picked up by a US submarine.

Of his two crewmates, one never made it out of the plane. The other's parachute failed to open and he plummeted to his death.

Eight flyboys besides Bush survived the downing of their planes, only to wind up as prisoners of war. Later war crimes testimony revealed these eight were also heroes, brave much longer than an extra five minutes, for all endured beatings and other torture before being executed. Four of them were eaten by their captors, their livers and thigh meat served as part of a dinner for senior Japanese officers.

How does it affect a young man, just twenty years old, to stare death in the face while flying a plane with its engine on fire? To watch a buddy fall to his death in the sea, an unopened parachute his death shroud? To set out on a mission as part of a team – and to return alone?

Years later, Bush told an interviewer for a CNN documentary that he thinks about his comrades all the time and while still on the submarine, began questioning his own survival. *"I have survivor's curiosity, I guess…Why had I been spared and what did God have in store for me? In my own view, there's got to be some kind of destiny and I was being spared for something on Earth."*

***

Three weeks after he returned from his tour in the Pacific, George Bush married his teenage sweetheart, Barbara Pierce, and had six children with her in thirteen years. He completed a degree from Yale in an accelerated program and captained his university baseball team during two College World Series—all while a husband and father of young children. After graduation, he started a successful oil business in

Texas and then, in 1964, entered politics. Over the years, he served as a U.S. congressman, ambassador, head of the CIA, and vice president under Ronald Reagan for eight years.

In 1988, Bush forged a winning campaign for the White House based on his vice-presidential experience, especially in foreign affairs. He was tasked with guiding the country during internationally uncertain times: Tiananmen Square, the fall of the Berlin Wall, the reunification of Germany and, most importantly, the dissolution of the Soviet Union. He sought to lead America's responses with conservative restraint and diplomacy. In Panama, with "Operation Just Cause," and in the Persian Gulf War, with "Operation Desert Storm," he achieved the goal she set out with a minimal loss of lives. Operation Desert Storm had a regrettable 148 casualties – but only 148.

Domestically, Bush was credited with the formation of "A Thousand Points of Light" to coordinate volunteerism to address social problems. In 1990, he was credited with passing the Clean Air Act Amendments, as well as the far-reaching Americans with Disabilities Act, which extended important benefits and accommodations to forty-three million Americans.

Overall, however, his handling of domestic issues met with less success than did his handling of foreign policy issues. His reneging on his "Read My Lips – No New Taxes," proved disastrous.

As a twenty-year-old pilot, George Bush, Sr. had been flying high when suddenly shot down over the Pacific. As President of the United States, he had been flying high on the strength of foreign diplomacy when unexpectedly shot down by domestic problems. Despite strong achievements abroad and at one point, a near-record-high approval rating of 89%, the American people did not return George H. W. Bush to office for a second term.

CHAPTER 16

George W. Bush
(1946 – present)

Eight years later, his son George W. Bush climbed into the pilot seat to guide the country as its 43rd president. Less than nine months in, he faced the first crisis of his presidency – the 9/11 terrorist attacks, the likes of which our country had never before seen. "The Decider," as he called himself, swung into action and his responses earned him praise. Seeking to address Americans' fears, he launched the War on Terrorism abroad and organized domestic means to combat terrorism, including pushing for a new Cabinet department, the U.S. Department of Homeland Security (DHS). This involved a massive government reorganization, absorbing twenty-two individual government agencies into a single organization.

But few of the actions taken to safeguard our country against further terrorist acts have been without controversy. Does the USA

PATRIOT Act offer better protection to our citizens or compromise their civil liberties? Over the course of two terms, the wars waged in Afghanistan and Iraq became more and more problematic, with their controversial origins and unsettled results.

Similar questions can be asked regarding the success and long-term impact of other programs and policy decisions. Did his tax cuts help or hurt the economy? Was the No Child Left Behind initiative effective? Was Medicare D effectively designed?

When approval ratings fluctuate between an all-time low of 19% and an astounding high of 92%, it clearly indicates a complicated presidency. George W himself once said, *"The true history of my administration will be written 50 years from now, and you and I will not be around to see it."*

While it will take some time for historians to sort through and reach a consensus among the conflicting assessments of George W's foreign and domestic policies, there is one decision "The Decider" made whose far-reaching positive effects can be noted.

In a July 26, 2012 article for the Washington Post, African-American columnist Eugene Robinson praised George W for his commitment to fighting AIDS in Africa. Going against the advice offered by others, he increased the US commitment to billions of dollars to provide antiretroviral medicine to more than 4 million men, women, and children infected with AIDS on the African subcontinent.

Robinson stated, *"…if Africa is gaining ground against AIDS, history will note that it was Bush, more than any other individual, who turned the tide. The man who called himself the Decider will be held accountable for a host of calamitous decisions. But for opening his heart to Africa, he deserves nothing but gratitude and praise."*

***

George W's mother, Barbara Bush, was almost universally regarded as likable and down-to-earth. She carried a few extra pounds. She didn't dye her snow-white hair. She was acquainted with tragedy and grief, particularly the gut-wrenching pain of burying a four-year-old daughter, Robin, who died of leukemia. She worked for universal literacy, and authored two children's books about her dogs, C. Fred and Millie. She was loyal, family-oriented, and had a strong marriage of an astounding 73 years' duration.

The male Bush dynasty, including her husband and sons, George and Jeb, perhaps not universally loved, but their aggregate influence on the course of American history cannot be denied. Over the course of four generations, the Bush family has given our country governors, a senator, a two-term vice president, and two presidents who served for a combined twelve years. Like the Kennedys before them, if the power of the dynasty has faded, its important role in our country's history cannot be denied.

Epilogue

I like to imagine some of John Howland's more famous descendants seated around a long Thanksgiving dinner table, John and Elizabeth presiding at either end. Would they feel pride as they looked around the table? Consternation? Perhaps a mixture of both?

Phillips Brooks and George H. W. Bush are discussing changes in the Episcopal church. Emerson is seated next to Joseph Smith. Emerson approves of Joseph Smith's following his own inner spiritual voice, but is less enamored with the religious dynasty that grew out of it.

Edith Roosevelt is reminiscing with her children. Longfellow and his children have joined them. One of Edith's children is reciting Longfellow's "The Midnight Ride of Paul Revere." There is laughter all around.

Dr. Benjamin Spock looks in their direction and nods with approval. He remembers Longfellow's comment, *"A torn coat is soon mended but harsh words bruise a child"* and thinks to himself, *Even before I published my book, he knew – he understood.*

But as someone passes him the turkey, Spock quickly keeps it moving, having converted to a totally vegan, macrobiotic diet. After a lifetime of giving advice, will he now be able to resist lecturing the others on the evils of eating meat?

Maude Adams is listening with rapt attention as Humphrey Bogart, Christopher Lloyd, and the Baldwin brothers discuss film.

George W. Bush, Sarah Palin, and FDR are arguing politics. Thank goodness someone had the foresight to seat Ruth du Pont at the other end of the table.

It's like every American family, writ large, with members seated around the Thanksgiving table talking, eating, laughing, reminiscing – and debating.

Would we be better or worse off if John Howland had drowned and none of these famous descendants had ever existed? Few of the aforementioned are universally acclaimed or vilified, but their impact on the national and international landscape is unmistakable. What we can say with certainty is that without them, it would be a different world from the one we now live in. No copies of *Baby and Child Care* on the shelves of 50 million homes. No Social Security. No "O Little Town of Bethlehem" at Christmas time. Perhaps no White House as we know it today.

And the final outcome of World War II without either FDR or Winston Churchill?

Kings, presidents, and generals shape history, but so do ordinary people, perhaps more than we realize. From Nietzche to children rescued from polio and AIDS, countless individuals have had their lives touched by some descendant of John and Elizabeth Tilley Howland.

Yes, John *and* Elizabeth. John Howland's legacy of presidents, philosophers, theologians, authors, and actors would never have been possible if Elizabeth Tilley had not also survived the voyage and that first winter; had not married him; had not become his stalwart, resourceful partner in raising their large family together.

A generation back there is also John Howland's mother, Margaret.

She lived in a small English village and bore fourteen children. No doubt she was largely uneducated, and knew both backbreaking work and grinding poverty. At least three of her sons had to make their way in the world as indentured servants, but those same three sons worked their way out of servitude and they – and she through them – have played a part in the shaping and governing of one of the mightiest nations history has ever known. Had John drowned on the voyage over, his brothers likely would not have followed, but he didn't, and so on they came, making their own marks in this new country. Whereas John's descendants include Presidents Franklin D. Roosevelt, George H. W. Bush and George W. Bush, his brothers Arthur and Henry have Presidents Ford and Nixon and Prime Minister Winston Churchill among their descendants. Four of Margaret Howland's descendants are listed in Smithsonian's 2015 magazine among the 100 Most Significant Americans of all time.

Not a bad legacy.

As poet William Ross Wallace once said, *"The hand that rocks the cradle rules the world."*

***

Grab, yank. Grab, yank.

Their clothes plastered to their bodies by the pouring rain, blood from their raw palms soaking the rough rope, the small band of sailors worked hand-over-hand to pull Margaret Howland's son, a poor indentured servant, up and over the railing.

How long did their rescue take? Probably no more than fifteen or twenty minutes. John Howland must have felt heavy as they worked to bring him back on board. Little did they realize that it might be more than his sea-soaked clothes and boots: like invisible barnacles, clinging to John Howland was the weight of millions of future descendants and the future of a new nation as yet unshaped, but waiting in the wings of history to rise like an eagle and take flight.

These coarse, uneducated sailors played a part in that history too, although history fails to record their names. Even nameless, the results of their action echo down through the centuries.

The echo reverberates under my own roof.

***

Her blonde pigtails stick straight out from the sides of her head. Fine, wispy things, they frequently slip out of the tiny rubber bands, for their owner is in constant motion.

She is sturdy, curious, a hard worker. The task of taking something apart and putting it back together can absorb all of her concentration for a surprisingly long period of time.

My two-year-old granddaughter, Elisabeth Tilley.

She has a brand-new little sister, Margaret Louise Anne. Although Margaret is named for her great-grandmother, Margaret Louise Howard, in her name there is a nod to another grandmother, fourteen generations back.

What will these newly-minted Howland women accomplish in their lifetimes? It's a shrinking world, through technology and travel getting smaller every day. Their parents are raising them tri-lingually, to prepare them for new realities. Will these girls make their marks in small but important ways, as have so many of their Howland ancestors, or will their talents shine on the national or international stage?

Only time will tell.

The story of John Howland illustrates both the importance of a single life and the wonderful tangled web of humanity. Each life important in its own way: Margaret, John, Elizabeth, the sailors, the Native people who helped them through that first winter. Ralph, Henry, Edith, Esther, Franklin, George; whether named or unnamed, each playing a part.

And on and on it goes. Millions of stories flowing from the original one, the collection of them more vast than the Atlantic that once threatened to swallow them all up.

Threatened to, before being thwarted by ordinary people.

A Compendium of Quotes

John Howland's descendants are a quotable lot, full of pithy wisdom.

Maude Adams

- I thought I was an odd person, and since my hometown had only about 70,000 people in it, I knew I was going to have to leave there and go out and find other odd people.
- Modeling is a great beginning but it's also kind of a trap if you have any ambition or a mind that needs to be stimulated.
- Don't be afraid of failure; be afraid of petty success.
- Don't let anyone persuade you that anything we do in life less than our own best is a worthy thing. You must never compromise with your life. We know when we are doing first-rate things. When we satisfy ourselves with second-rate things, it is the beginning of a long, long death.

Humphrey Bogart

- A hot dog at the ballpark beats roast beef at the Ritz.
- All you owe the public is a good performance.
- Here's lookin' at you, kid. (Casablanca 1942)
- We'll always have Paris. (Casablanca, 1942)
- I think this may be the beginning of a beautiful friendship. (Casablanca, 1942)

- Things are never so bad they can't be made worse. (The African Queen, 1951)
- It's the stuff dreams are made of. (Maltese Falcon, 1941)
- There's no sacrifice too great for a chance at immortality. (In a Lonely Place, 1950)

Phillips Brooks
- No man or woman can be strong, gentle, pure, and good, without the world being better for it and without someone being helped and comforted by the very existence of that goodness.
- Christianity helps us face the music even when we don't like the tune.
- I do not pray for a lighter load, but for a stronger back.
- Set yourself earnestly to see what you are made to do, and then set yourself earnestly to do it.
- Sad will be the day for any man when he becomes contented with the thoughts he is thinking and the deeds he is doing - where there is not forever beating at the doors of his soul some great desire to do something larger, which he knows he was meant and made to do.
- Character may be manifested in the great moments, but it is made in the small ones.
- The true way to be humble is not to stoop until you are smaller than yourself, but to stand at your real height against some higher nature that will show you what the real smallness of your greatness is.

- Do not pray for tasks equal to your powers. Pray for powers equal to your tasks.
- Be such a man, and live such a life, that if every man were such as you, and every life a life like yours, this earth would be God's Paradise.
- Forgive, forget. Bear with the faults of others as you would have them bear with yours.
- A prayer in its simplest definition is merely a wish turned Godward.
- The ideal life is in our blood and never will be still.
- Do not pray for easy lives. Pray to be stronger men!
- No man has come to true greatness who has not felt that his life belongs to his race, and that which God gives to him, He gives him for mankind.
- It does not take great men to do great things; it only takes consecrated men.
- The man who has begun to live more seriously within begins to live more simply without.
- Charity should begin at home, but should not stay there.

George H. W. Bush
- Every loss of life is terrible.
- I can tell you this: if I am ever in a position to call the shots, I'm not going to rush to send somebody else's kids into a war.
- I'll be glad to respond to or dodge your questions, depending on what I think will help our election most.

- That's a very good question, very direct, and I'm not going to answer it.
- I think in defeat you grope for things that are happy, and it's hard.
- It's much worse to read criticism about your son than yourself.
- The day will come – and it is not far off – when the legacy of Lincoln will finally be fulfilled at 1600 Pennsylvania Avenue, when a black man or woman will sit in the Oval Office. When that day comes, the most remarkable thing about it will be how naturally it occurs.
- We are not the sum of our possessions.
- A new breeze is blowing, and a world refreshed by freedom seems reborn; for in man's heart, if not in fact, the day of the dictator is over. The totalitarian era is passing, its old ideas blown away like leaves from an ancient, lifeless tree.
- Aging's alright, better than the alternative, which is not being here.
- We don't want an America that's closed to the world. What we want is a world that is open to America.
- America is never wholly herself unless she is engaged in high moral principle. We as a people have such a purpose today. It is to make kinder the face of the nation and gentler the face of the world.
- We are a nation of communities…a brilliant diversity spread like stars, like a thousand points of light in a broad and peaceful sky.

- I have opinions of my own, strong opinions, but I don't always agree with them.
- I'm a conservative, but I'm not a nut about it.
- I do not like broccoli. And I haven't liked it since I was a kid and my mother made me eat it. I'm President of the United States and I'm not going to eat any more broccoli.
- What's wrong with being a boring kind of guy?
- I like a colorful sock. I'm a sock man.

George W. Bush

- We will not waiver; we will not tire; we will not falter; we will not fail. Peace and Freedom will prevail.
- We will build new ships to carry man forward into the universe, to gain a new foothold on the moon, and to prepare for new journeys to the worlds beyond our own.
- Today we affirm a new commitment to live out our nation's promise through civility, courage, compassion, and character.
- I believe that God has planted in every heart the desire to live in freedom.
- Everywhere that freedom stirs, let tyrants fear.
- Use power to help people. For we are given power, not to advance our own purposes nor to make a great show in the world, nor a name. There is but one just use of power and it is to serve people.

- To those of you who received honors, awards, and distinctions, I say well done. And to the "C" students, I say you, too, can be president of the United States.
- Some folks look at me and see a certain swagger, which in Texas is called "walking."
- America is the land of the second chance – and when the gates of the prison open, the path ahead should lead to a better life.
- You can spend your money better than the government can spend your money.

Florence Earle Coates
- Beauty is eternal and ugliness, thank God, is ephemeral. Can there be any question as to which should attract the poet?
- The business of art is to enlarge and correct the heart and to lift our ideals out of the ugly and the mean through love of the ideal. The business of art is to appeal to the soul.
- A man's wisdom is measured by his hope.
- Fear is the fire that melts Icarian wings.

Ralph Waldo Emerson
- Hitch your wagon to a star.
- We aim above the mark to hit the mark.
- Enthusiasm is the mother of effort, and without it nothing great was ever achieved.
- America is another name for opportunity.

- As a cure for worrying, work is better than whiskey.
- It is one of the beautiful compensations in this life that no one can help another without helping himself.
- Every actual State is corrupt. Good men must not obey laws too well.
- It was high counsel that I once heard given to a young person, "always do what you are afraid to do."
- Do the thing we fear, and the death of fear is sure.
- If you would lift me up, you must be on higher ground.
- Every experiment, of multitudes or individuals, that has a sensual and selfish aim, will fail.
- Build a better mousetrap and the world will beat a path to your door.
- Make yourself necessary to someone.
- Knowledge is knowing that we cannot know.
- No great man complains of want of opportunity.
- A man is usually more careful of his money than of his principles.
- Can anything be so elegant as to have few wants, and to serve them oneself?
- A man builds a fine house, and now he has a master, and a task, for life; he has to furnish, watch, show it, and keep it in repair the rest of his days.
- Nothing astonishes men so much as common sense and plain dealing.
- Men love to wonder, and that is the seed of science.
- Science does not know its debt to imagination.

- The invariable mark of wisdom is to see the miraculous in the common.
- Don't be too timid and squeamish about your actions. All life is an experiment.
- A foolish consistency is the hobgoblin of little minds, adored by little statesmen and philosophers and divines.
- There was never a child so lovely but his mother was glad to get him to sleep.
- We are always getting ready to live but never living.
- No change of circumstances can repair a defect of character.
- As we grow old, the beauty steals inward.
- The greatest gift is a portion of thyself.
- We are rich only through what we give, and poor only through what we refuse.
- Every artist was first an amateur.
- What is a weed? A plant whose virtues have never been discovered.
- The earth laughs in flowers.
- Shallow men believe in luck. Strong men believe in cause and effect.
- Money often costs too much.
- For everything you have missed, you have gained something else, and for everything you gain, you lose something else.
- Write it on your heart that every day is the best day in the year.
- A great man is always willing to be little.
- Fear defeats more people than any other one thing in the

world.
- Common sense is genius dressed in its working clothes.
- An ounce of action is worth a ton of theory.
- Win as if you were used to it, lose as if you enjoyed it for a change.
- We gain the strength of the temptation we resist.
- It is not the length of life, but the depth of life.
- Never lose an opportunity of seeing something beautiful, for beauty is God's handwriting.
- To be yourself in a world that is constantly trying to make you something else is the greatest accomplishment.
- The only way to have a friend is to be one.
- It is one of the blessings of old friends, that you can afford to be stupid with them.
- The creation of a thousand forests is in one acorn.
- For every minute you remain angry, you give up sixty seconds of peace of mind.
- The greatest glory in living lies not in never failing, but in rising every time we fall.
- Though we travel the world over to find the beautiful, we must carry it with us or we find it not.
- Our chief want is someone who will inspire us to be what we know we could be.
- The age of a woman doesn't mean a thing. The best tunes are played on the oldest fiddles.
- All I have seen teaches me to trust the creator for all I have not seen.

- He who is not every day conquering some fear has not learned the secret of life.
- The first wealth is health.
- The end of the human race will be that it will eventually die of civilization.
- Love of beauty is taste. The creation of beauty is art.
- Character is higher than intellect.
- The reward of a thing well done is having done it.
- Who you are speaks so loudly that I can't hear what you're saying.
- What lies behind you and what lies in front of you pales in comparison to what lies within you.
- You cannot do a kindness too soon, for you never know how soon it will be too late.

Eville Gorham
- My kind of science is based on chance and serendipity… my view is, I think this might be interesting, let's get some data and see what they tell us.
- There is reason for hope. It may seem unimaginable that we can learn to manage consciously the entire planetary ecosystem. We should, however, remember that throughout our relatively short history, the unimaginable has morphed into the commonplace.

Henry Wadsworth Longfellow
- A single conversation across the table with a wise man is

better than ten years mere study of books.
- A thought often makes us hotter than a fire.
- Perseverance is a great element of success. If you only knock long enough and loud enough at the gate, you are sure to wake up somebody.
- For age is opportunity no less than youth itself, though in another dress; and as the evening twilight fades away, the sky is filled with stars, invisible by day.
- No matter how things may seem, no evil thing is success and no good thing is failure.
- A torn coat is soon mended but harsh words bruise a child.
- Not in the clamor of the crowded street, not in the shouts and plaudits of the throng, but in ourselves, are triumph and defeat.
- He that respects himself is safe from others. He wears a coat of mail that none can pierce.
- If we could read the secret history of our enemies we should find in each man's life, sorrow and suffering enough to disarm all hostility.
- Every man has his secret sorrows which the world knows not; and often times we call a man cold when he is only sad.
- The great tragedy of the average man is that he goes to his grave with his music still in him.
- There is no grief like the grief that does not speak.
- The heart, like the mind, has a memory. And in it are kept the most precious keepsakes.

- Look not mournfully into the past, it comes not back again. Wisely improve the present, it is thine. Go forth to meet the shadowy future without fear and with a manly heart.
- Ah, how good it feels – the hand of an old friend!
- Music is the universal language of mankind – poetry their universal pastime and delight.
- We judge ourselves by what we feel capable of doing, while others judge us by what we have already done.
- It takes less time to do a thing right, than it does to explain why you did it wrong.
- Success is not something to wait for, it is something to work for.
- The talent of success is nothing more than doing what you can do, well.
- The life of a man consists not in seeing visions and in dreaming dreams, but in active charity and willing service.
- Enthusiasm begets enthusiasm.
- Great is the art of beginning, but greater the art of ending.
- The darker the night, the nearer the dawn.
- Silence and solitude, the soul's best friends.
- Glorious indeed is the world of God around us but more glorious is the world of God within us.
- The highest exercise of imagination is not to devise what has no existence, but rather to perceive what really exists, though unseen by the outward eye – not creation, but insight.
- Give what you have. To someone, it may be better than you

dare to think.
- Nature is a revelation of God; art a revelation of man.
- Know how sublime a thing it is to suffer and be strong.
- What discord we should bring into the universe if our prayers were all answered. Then we should govern the world and not God. And do you think we should govern it better? It gives me only pain when I hear the long, wearisome petitions of people asking for they know not what…Thanksgiving with a full heart – and the rest silence and submission to the divine will!
- If we love one another, nothing, in truth, can harm us, whatever mischances may happen.
- Everyone says that forgiveness is a lovely idea until he has something to forgive.
- Live up to the best that is in you: Live noble lives, as you all may, in whatever condition you may find yourselves.
- Today is the block with which we build.
- I am more afraid of deserving criticism than of receiving it.
- Youth comes but once a lifetime. Perhaps, but it remains strong in many for their entire lives.
- When we walk toward the sun of Truth, all shadows are cast behind us.
- Love keeps the cold out better than a cloak.
- The human voice is the organ of the soul.
- The spring came suddenly, bursting upon the world as a child bursts into a room, with a laugh and a shout and hands full of flowers.

- Art is the child of nature.
- When Christ ascended triumphantly from star to star, He left the gates of Heaven ajar.
- Being all fashioned of the self-same dust, let us be merciful, as well as just.
- All that is best in the great poets of all countries is not what is national in them, but what is universal.
- Joy, temperance, and repose, slam the door on the doctor's nose.
- Love gives itself; it's not bought.
- I do not believe anyone can be perfectly well, who has a brain and a heart.
- Taste the joy that springs from labor.
- Whatever poet, orator, or sage may say of it, old age is still old age.
- Dreams or illusions, call them what you will; they lift us from the commonplace of life to better things.
- Time is the life of the soul.
- Let us then be up and doing.
- I love the author more for having himself been a lover of books.
- Hope has many lives as a cat or a king.

Be still, sad heart! And cease repining;
Behind the clouds is the sun still shining;
Thy fate is the common fate of all,
Into each life some rain must fall.

***

Kind hearts are the garden, kind thoughts the roots;
Kind words are the flowers, kind deeds the fruits.
Take care of your garden and keep out the weeds;
Fill it with sunshine, kind words, and kind deeds.

***

Each morning sees some task begun,
each evening sees it close;
Something attempted, something done;
has earned a night's repose.

***

Edith Roosevelt

- "One cannot bring up boys to be eagles and then expect them to be sparrows."
- I think imagination is one of the greatest blessings of life, and as long as one can lose oneself in a book, one can never be thoroughly unhappy.

Franklin Delano Roosevelt

- The only thing we have to fear is fear itself.
- Yesterday, December seventh, 1941, is a day which will live in infamy…We will gain the inevitable triumph, so help us God.
- In our personal ambitions, we are individuals. But in our seeking for economic and political progress as a nation, we all go up – or we all go down as one people.

- The virtues are lost in self-interest as rivers are lost in the sea.
- Remember, you are just an extra in everyone else's play.
- A nation that destroys its soils, destroys itself. Forests are the lungs of our land, purifying the air and giving fresh strength to our people.
- It isn't sufficient just to want – you've got to ask yourself what you are going to do to get the things you want.
- This generation of Americans has a rendezvous with destiny.
- The truth is found when men are free to pursue it.
- The only sure bulwark of continuing liberty is a government strong enough to protect the interests of the people and a people strong enough and well enough informed to maintain its sovereign control over the government.
- Competition has been shown to be useful up to a certain point and no further but cooperation, which is the thing we must strive for today, begins where competition leaves off.
- We must especially beware of that small group of selfish men who would clip the wings of the American Eagle in order to feather their own nests.
- If civilization is to survive, we must cultivate the science of human relationships – the ability of all peoples, of all kinds, to live together, in the same world at peace.
- People acting together as a group can accomplish things which no individual acting alone could accomplish.
- Courage is not the absence of fear, but rather the assessment

that something else is more important than fear.
- Calm seas never made a good sailor.
- It is better to swallow words than have to eat them later.
- Rules are not necessarily sacred, principles are.
- Repetition does not transform a lie into truth.
- When you reach the end of your rope, tie a knot in it and hang on.

Joseph Smith, Jr.
- If we would secure and cultivate the love of others, we must love others, even our enemies as well as friends.
- Wise men ought to have understanding enough to conquer men with kindness.
- For a man to be great, he must not dwell on small things, though he may enjoy them.
- Never exact of a friend in adversity, what you would require in prosperity.

Benjamin Spock
- Parents' natural loving care for their children is most important.
- Have confidence in your abilities and trust your common sense.
- The surest way to raise mentally healthy children is to cultivate loving, nurturing, and mutually respectful relationships with them.
- Loving means, first of all, accepting your child as a person.

Every child has strengths and weaknesses, gifts and challenges.
- Loving means adjusting your expectations to fit your child, not trying to adjust your child to fit your expectations.

www.ingramcontent.com/pod-product-compliance
Lightning Source LLC
Chambersburg PA
CBHW070143080526
44586CB00015B/1822